Doodle All year

Taro Gomi

Doodle All year

Taro Gomi

chronicle books · san francisco

Spring

Color these butterflies as brightly as you can.

Color as many strawberries as you can eat!

Make a strawberry cake.

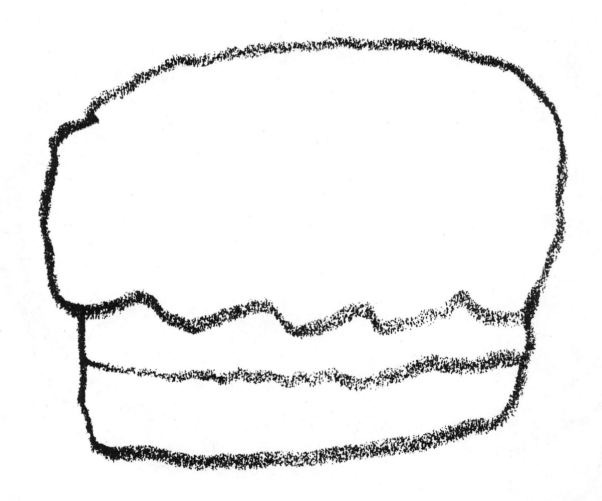

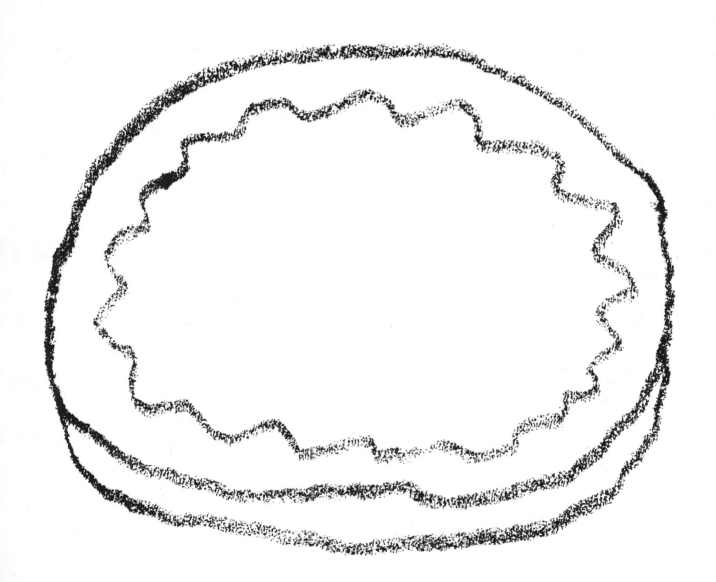

Cover these trees with green leaves.

This girl's best friend has moved away.
Draw her some new friends.

Can you draw friends for this boy, too?

Lots of birds live in this tree. Can you draw them?

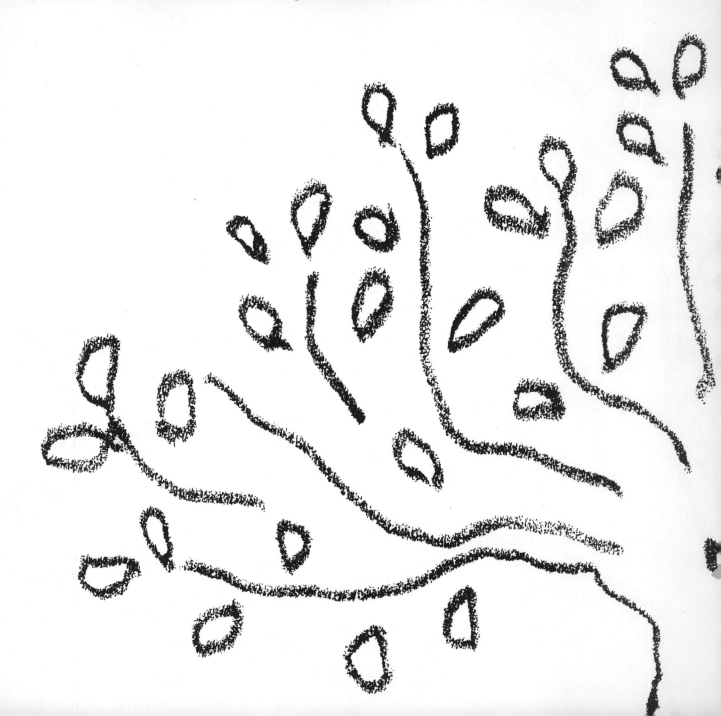

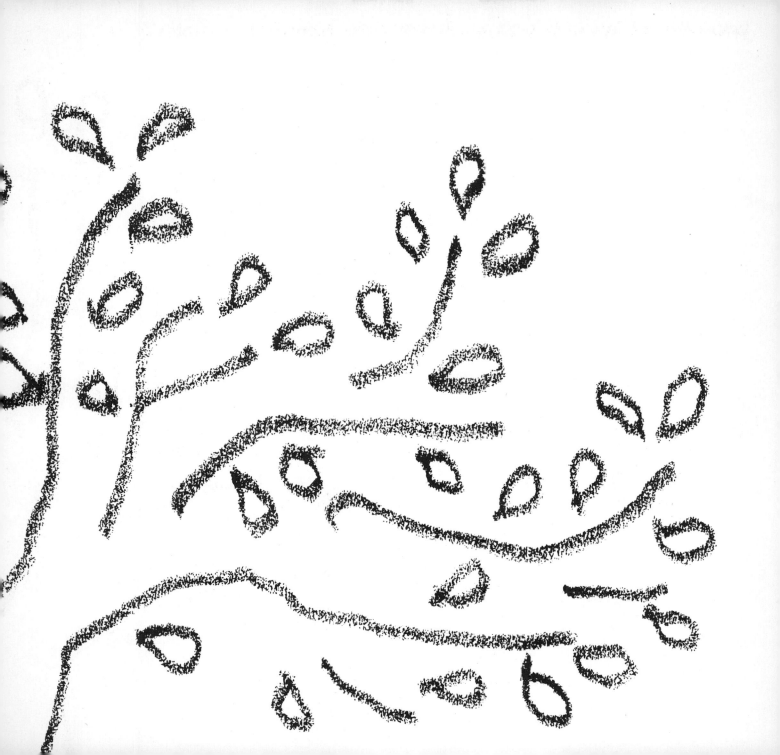

What other insects are poking their heads up from these holes?

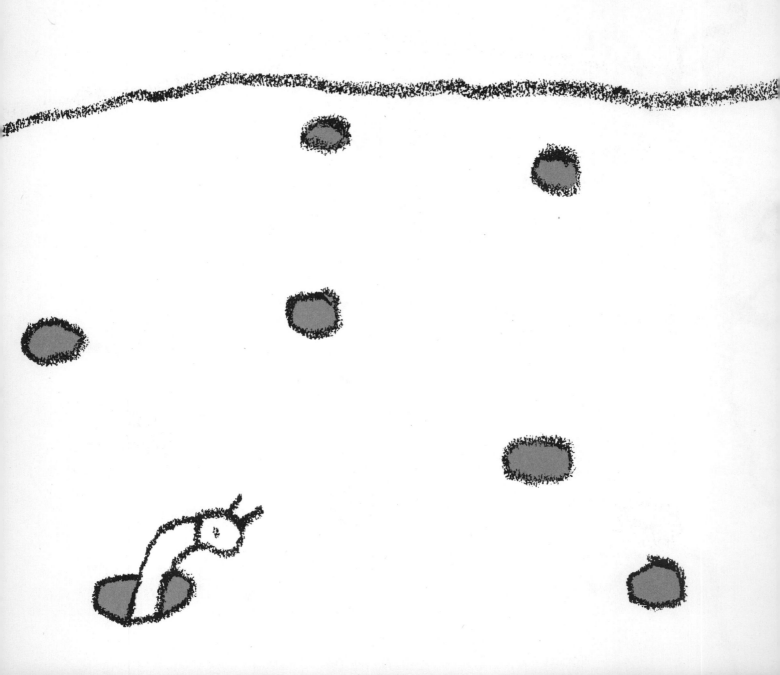

It's springtime!
Can you draw these kids some clothes for warm weather?

Draw fish swimming upstream.

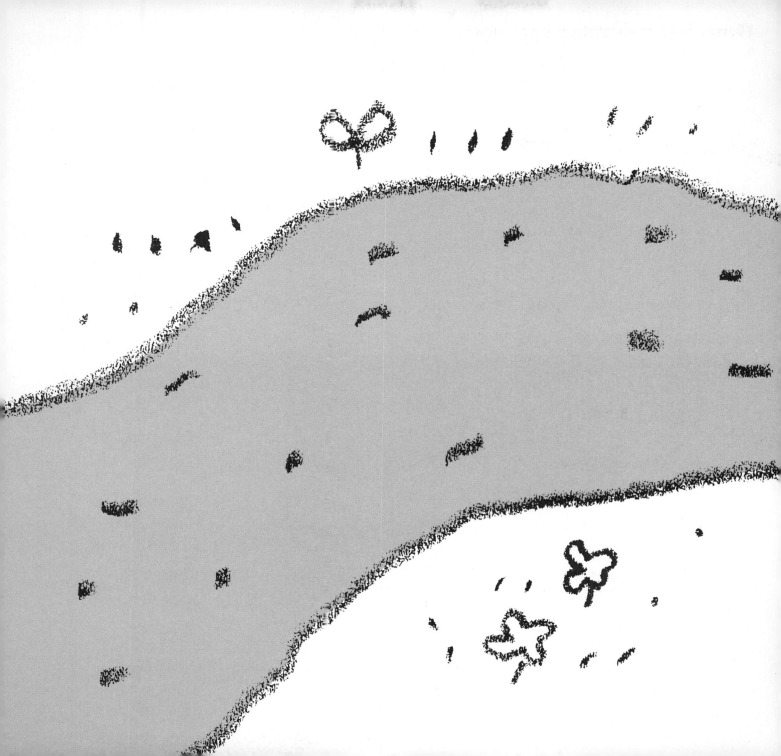

Here are some tulips. Can you color them?

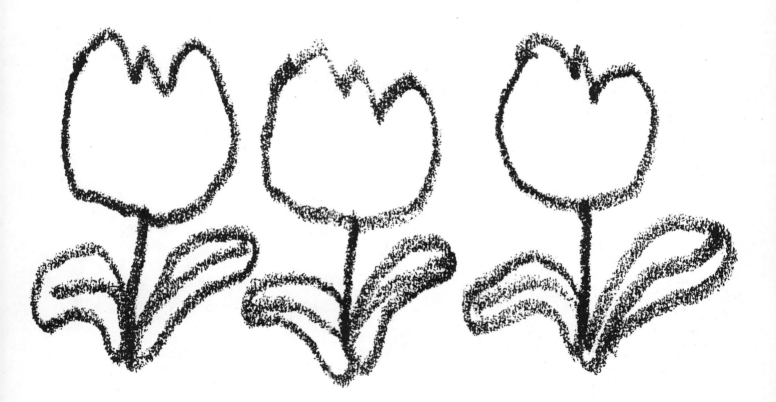

Here are some flowers.
Can you color them and draw their stems?

The wind is blowing away all the spring blossoms.
Can you catch them?

Achoo! It's the season for hay fever. Quick! Give them tissues.

Draw the people who live in this house.
Also, draw their cats taking naps in the sunshine.

Draw bees playing in these flowers.

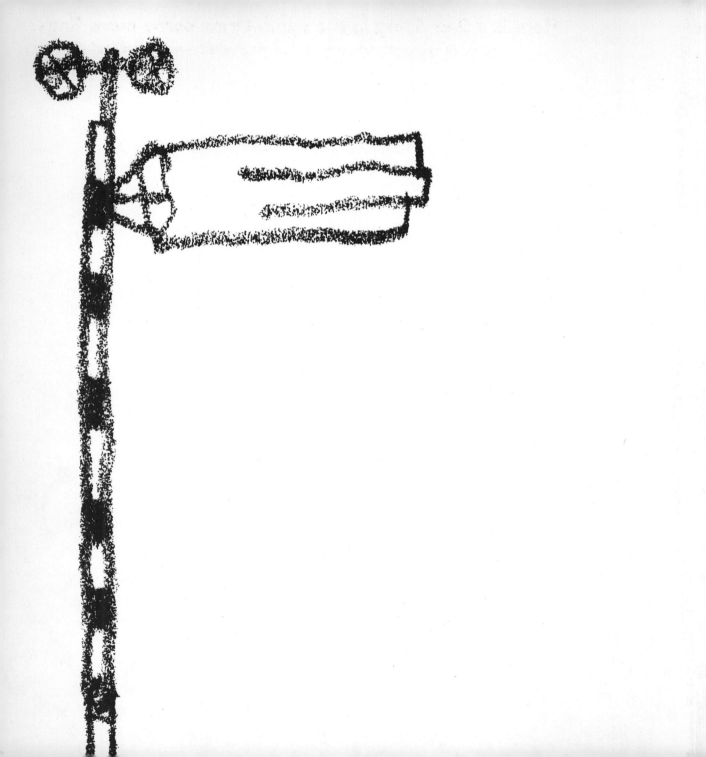

Here is a flag flying in the wind. Draw some more flags.
(You can make them any shape you want—even animal shapes.)

Draw some sea creatures swimming in the waves.

These seashells need colorful patterns.

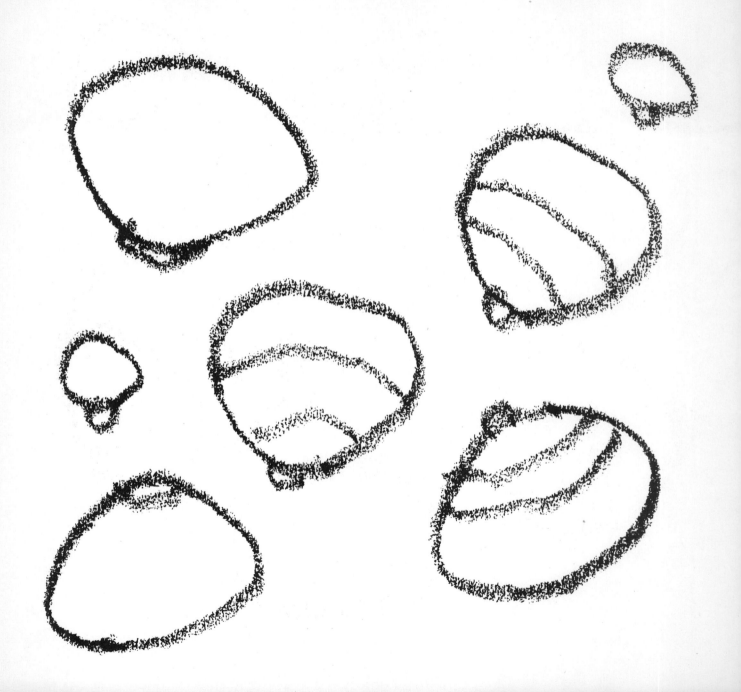

Color each bird so beautifully that no one will be able to decide which bird is prettier!

It's time for a walk.
What kind of dogs are these people walking?

Where is this bus going?

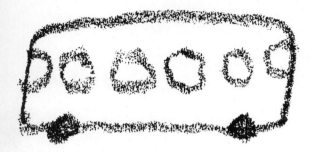

Where is this car going?

Draw some green, tasty grass for this goat and this cow.

Make these vegetables tasty colors.

Draw people walking.

**This polar bear and snowy owl are tired of being white.
Quick! Color them!**

Follow the leader! Draw children walking single file.

Draw a spring rain shower.

Draw hot air balloons floating over this town.

Now, draw an airplane flying over the town.

Now, draw a flying saucer!

Draw goldfish swimming in this fishbowl.

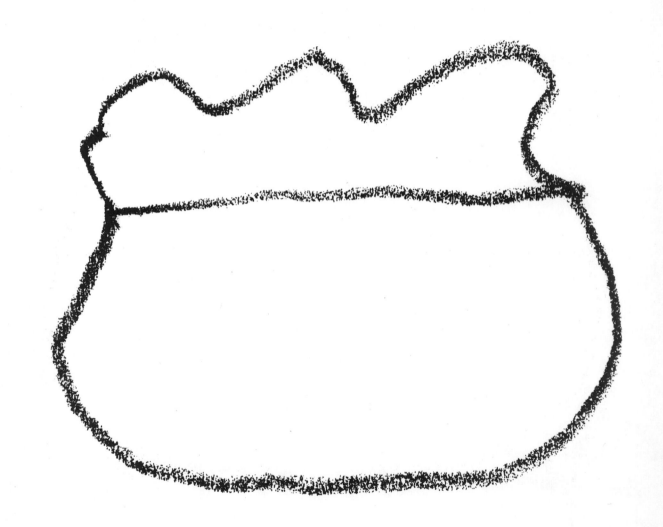

Draw brightly colored tropical fish swimming in this fishbowl.

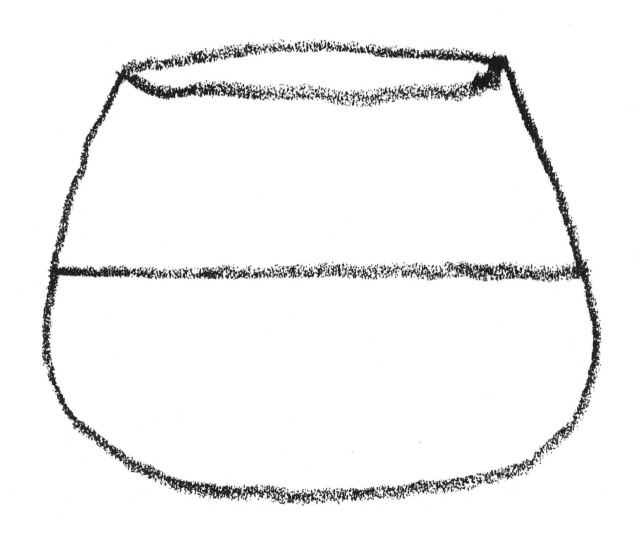

This little girl is taking her nap on a very comfortable bed.

But this little boy prefers to take his nap on the sofa.

Can you decorate these platters with spring colors
and fill them with delicious food?

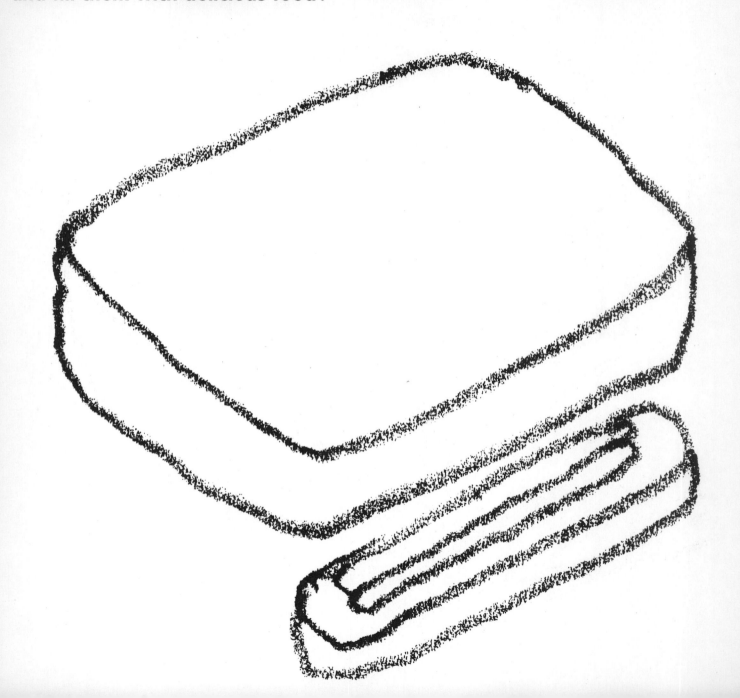

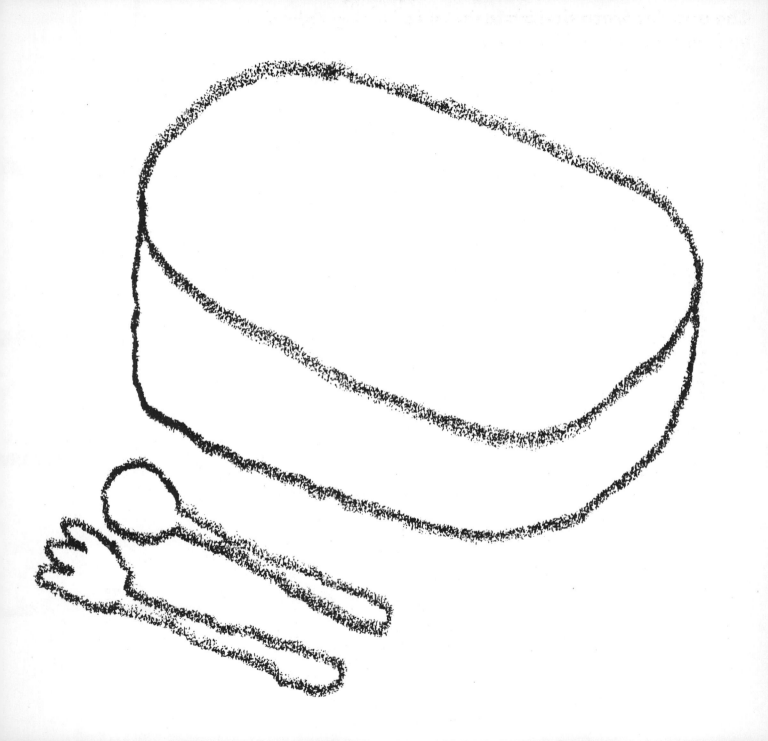

These crocodiles need spring outfits.

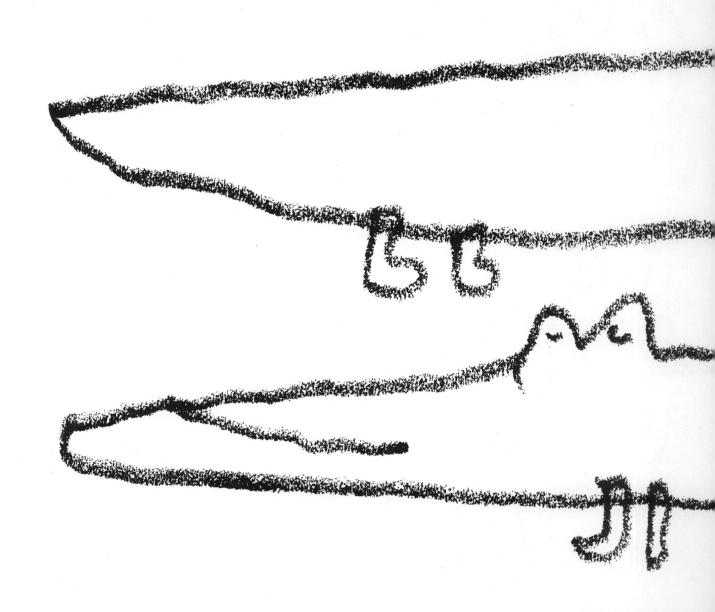

Draw people sitting on these park benches.

Grow some vegetables in this field.

What colors are the gems in these necklaces?

Tie lots of ribbons in these two girls' hair.

Draw children on this swing set. Did any of them fall off?

Uh-oh! Their ball is rolling down the hill!

What is your favorite kind of doughnut?

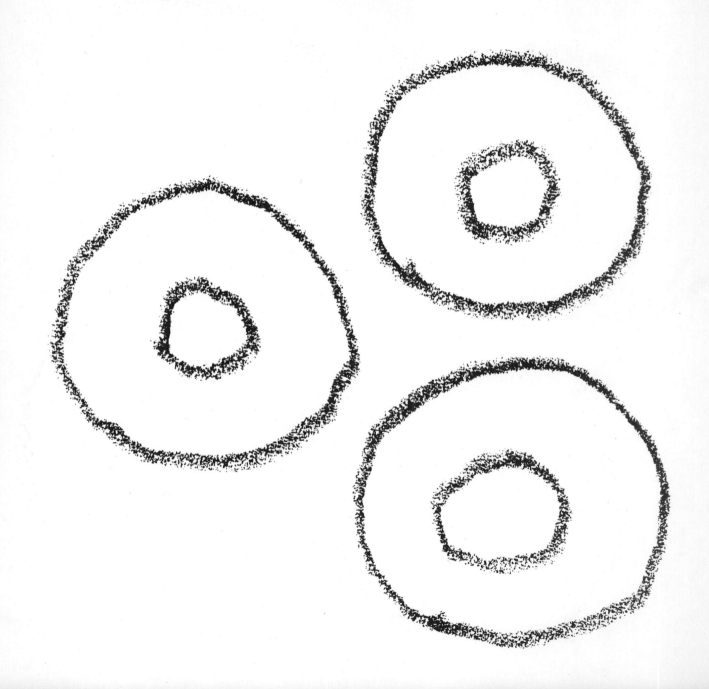

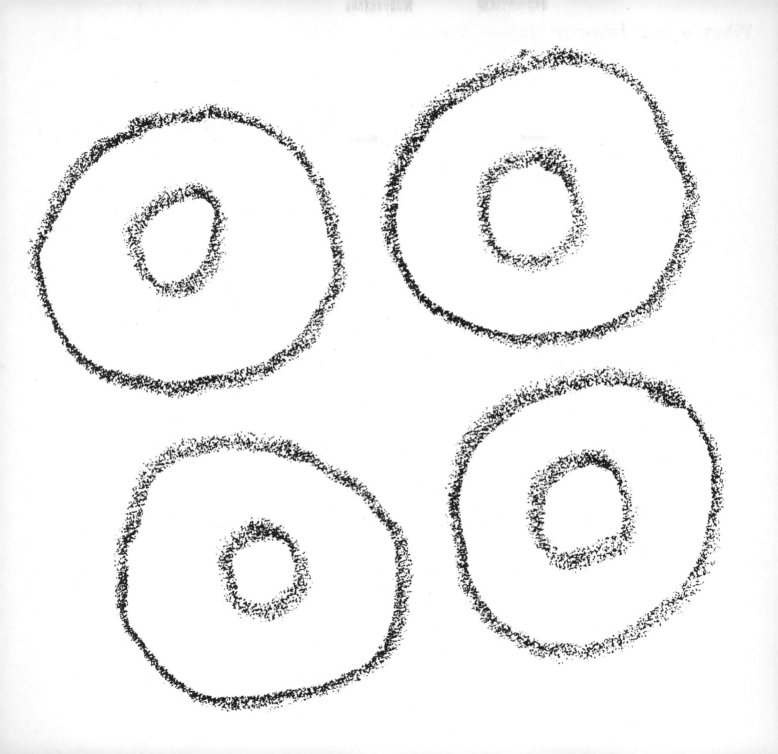

This boy is riding a bicycle—

These kids are having lots of fun! What do you think they are saying?

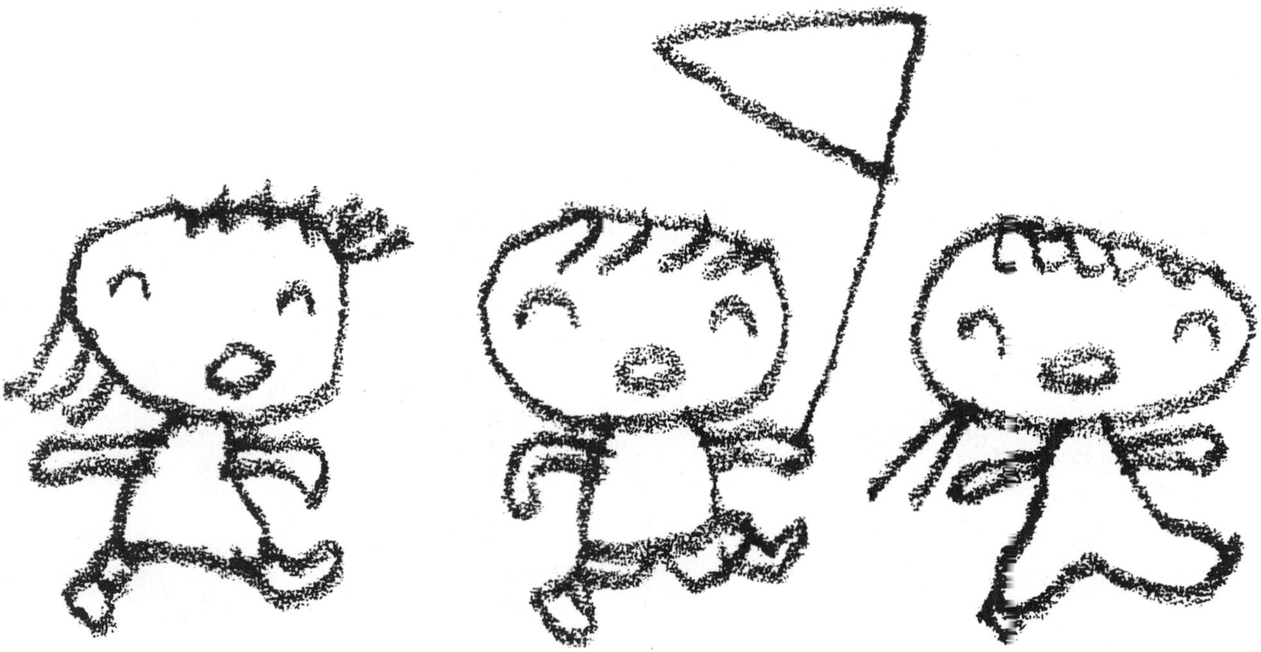

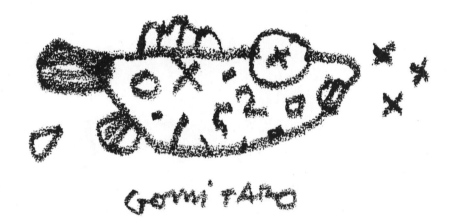

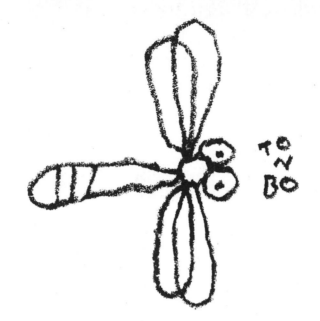

Summer

Here is a pale sun. Draw a really bright sun.

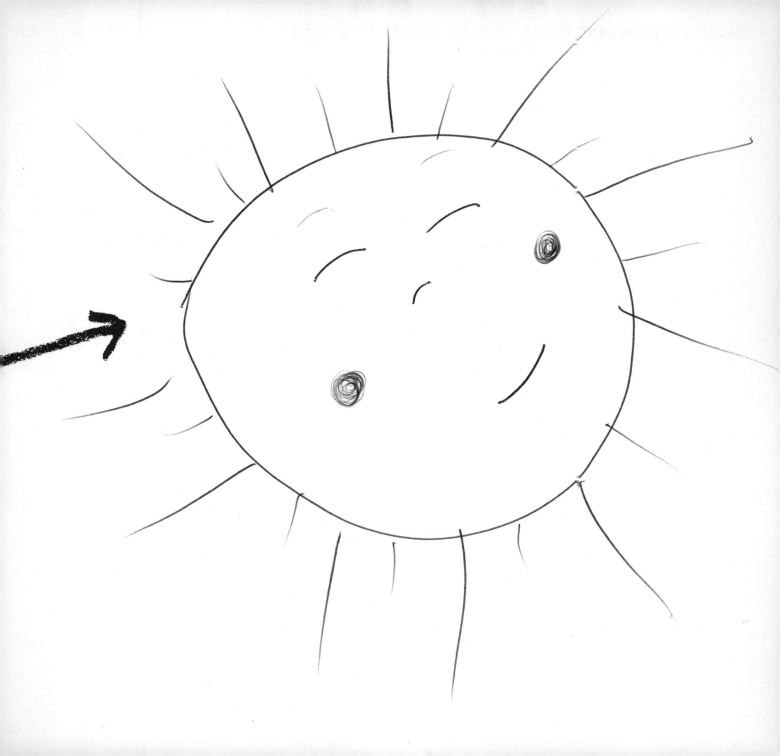

Draw a summer sky.

Color this watermelon.

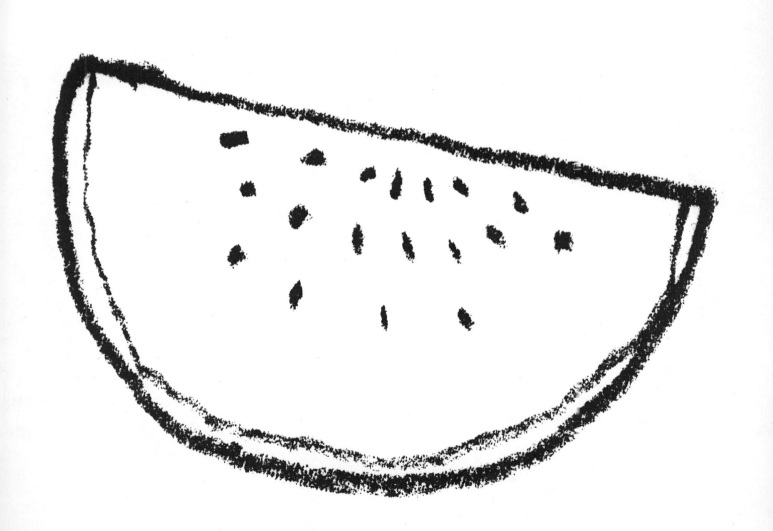

Draw storm clouds.

It's a water fight!

It's an elephant water fight!

Decorate these T-shirts.

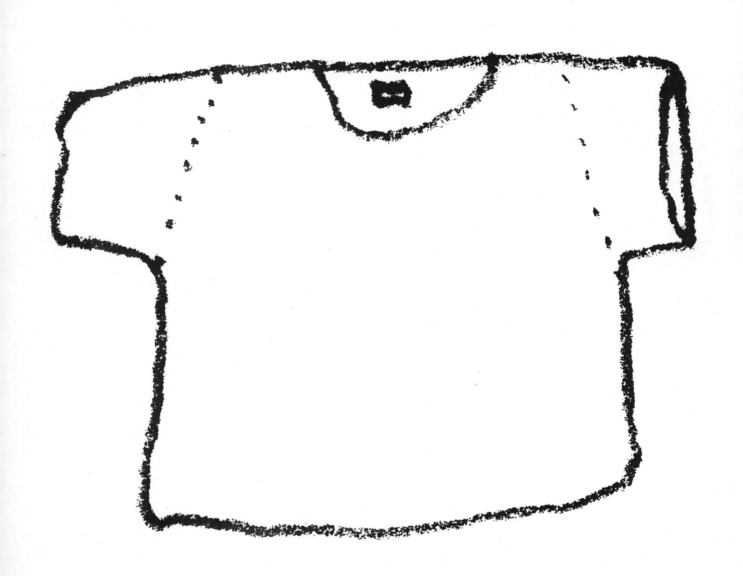

Decorate the kimonos of these Japanese children.

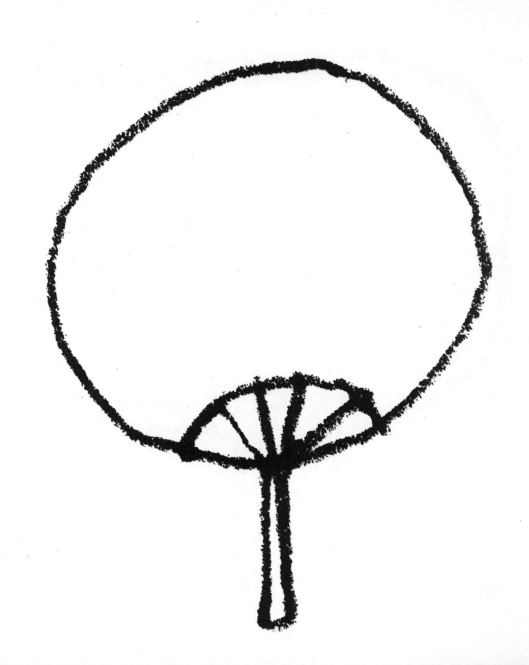

Here is a farm in the summertime.
Draw lots of animals in the field.

**These are the mountains in the summertime.
Draw people hiking and camping.**

Add blossoms to these sunflowers.

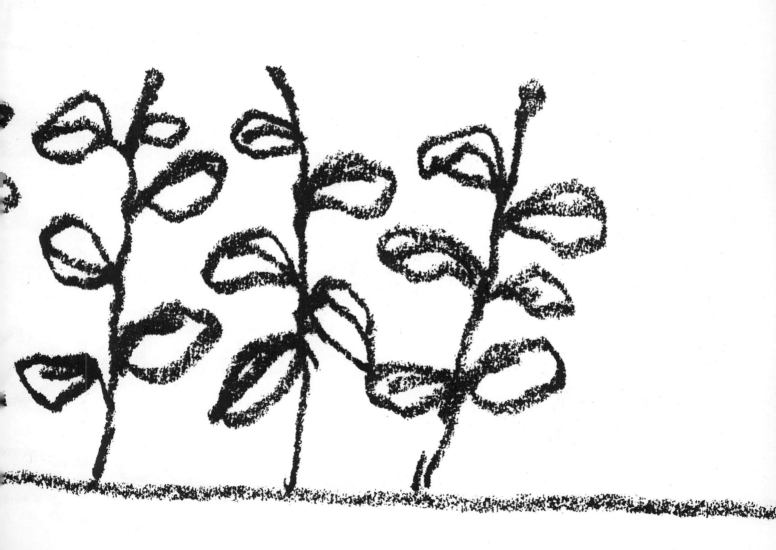

Add people to this beach.

Draw some surfers.

Draw deep-sea divers and sea creatures.

Put sunblock on these children.

It's too hot! Quick! Draw a hat on each child.

All these animals need sunglasses.

Draw lots of bugs in this grass.

Fill these huge bowls of ice cream with your favorite flavors.

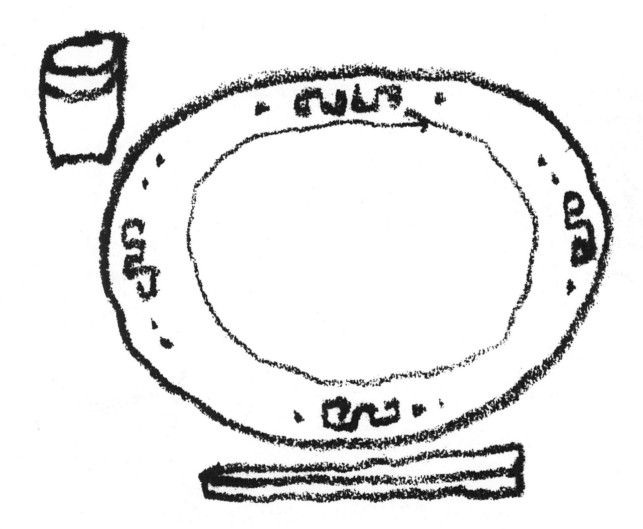

Fill this plate, too.

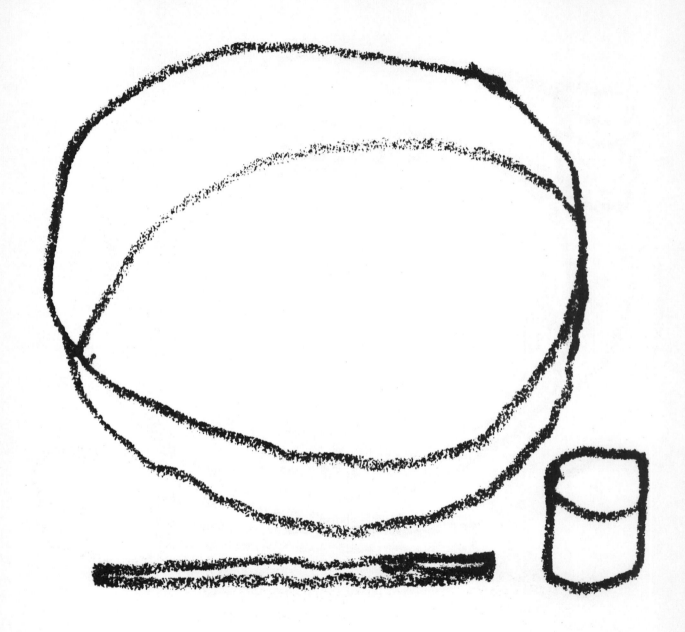

Fill these glasses with

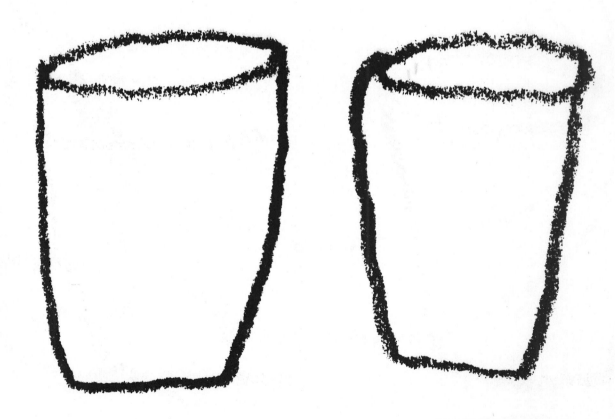

. . . orange juice   . . . lemonade

. . . iced tea   . . . soda pop!

It's the Fourth of July! Draw sparklers.

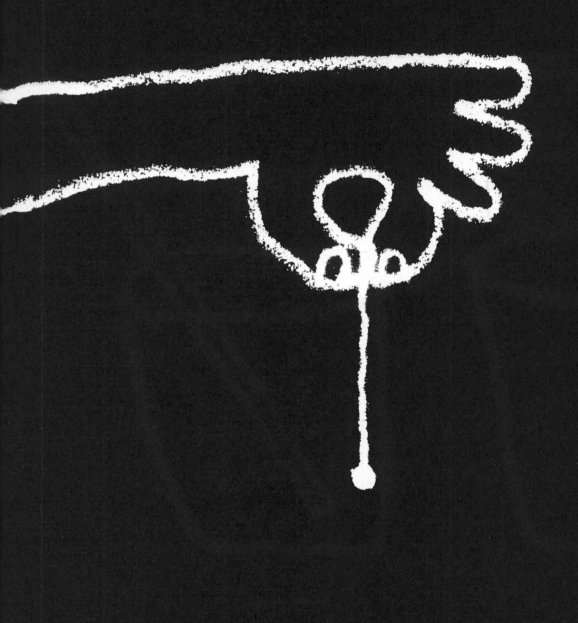

Here is a glowstick. Make it glow.

Draw fireworks in the night sky.

Light this mosquito coil. It will create a lot of smoke!

Draw a mosquito biting this child.

It's time to light the campfire.

Now it's time to put up the tent.

While you're at it, why not build a cabin?

It's hot today. Draw earthworms staying cool underground.

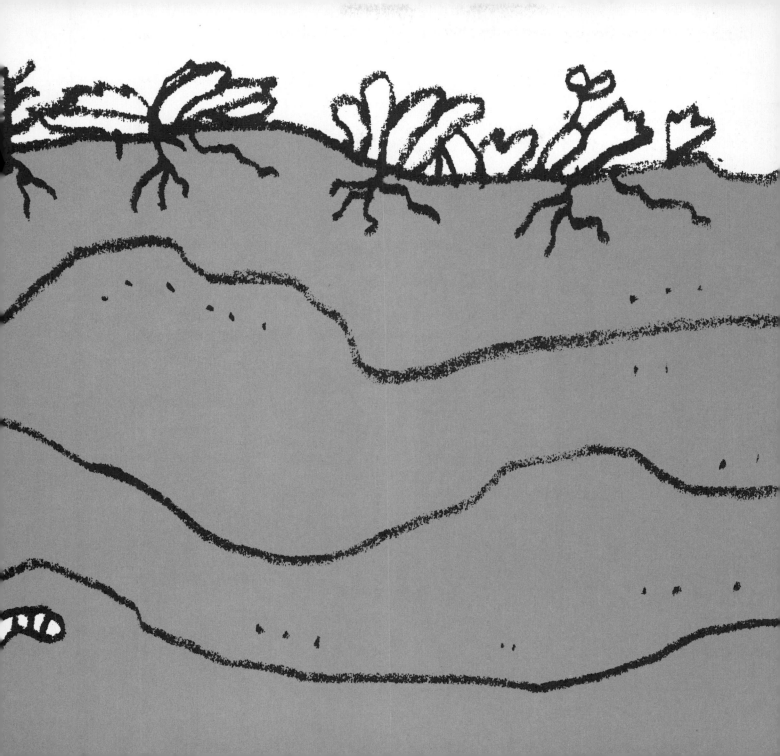

Draw fish swimming (very carefully) with this shark.

Draw camels in the desert.

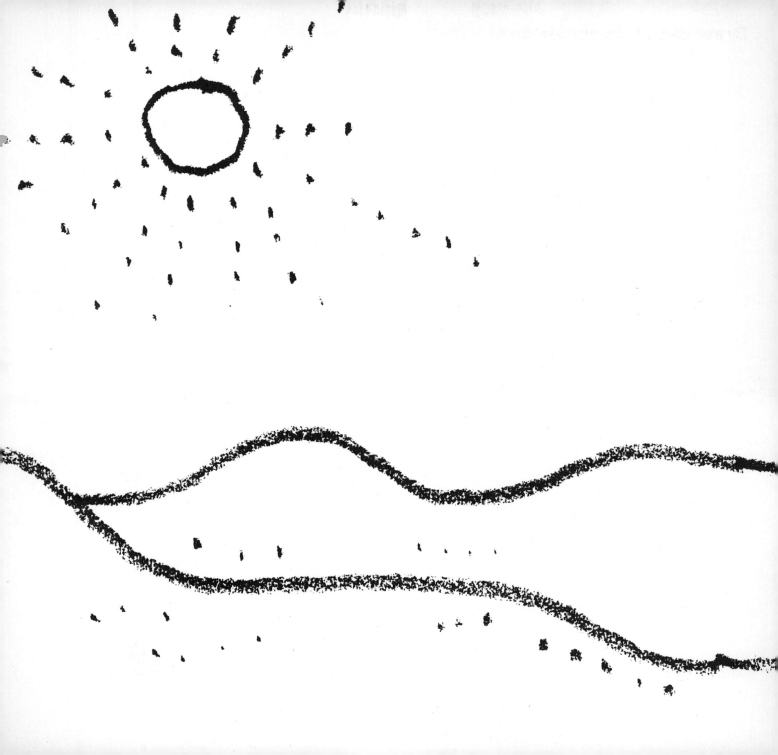

Draw lots of penguins on the ice.

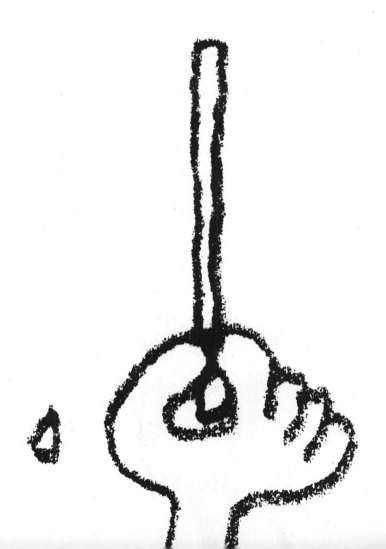

Can you fill this cone with ice cream?
(Your favorite flavor, of course.)

Draw a light, refreshing rain shower.

Uh-oh! It turned into a thunderstorm!
(Don't forget to draw the lightning!)

The storm has passed. Can you see a rainbow?

Hang some laundry out to dry.

These children are taking naps.
Can you cover them with blankets?

These animals need swimsuits.

Draw some scary ghosts.

Draw people relaxing in these hammocks.

Create some constellations in the summer sky.
(If you can find the Scorpion, you're a star!)

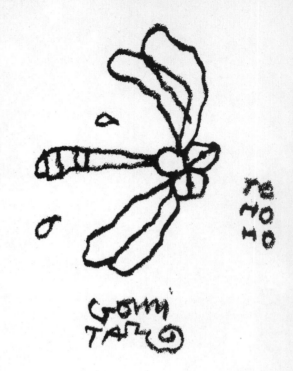

GONNI
TAN

2011

Fall

Color these autumn leaves.

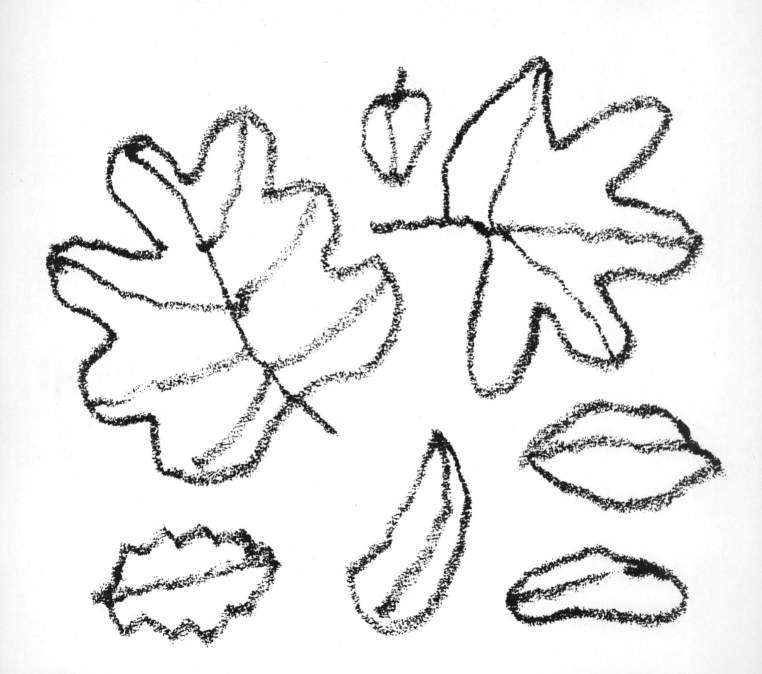

Draw paper airplanes in the sky.

Can you make more potato faces?

Tie pretty ribbons in this girl's hair.

Draw lots of falling leaves.

These dolls need heads!

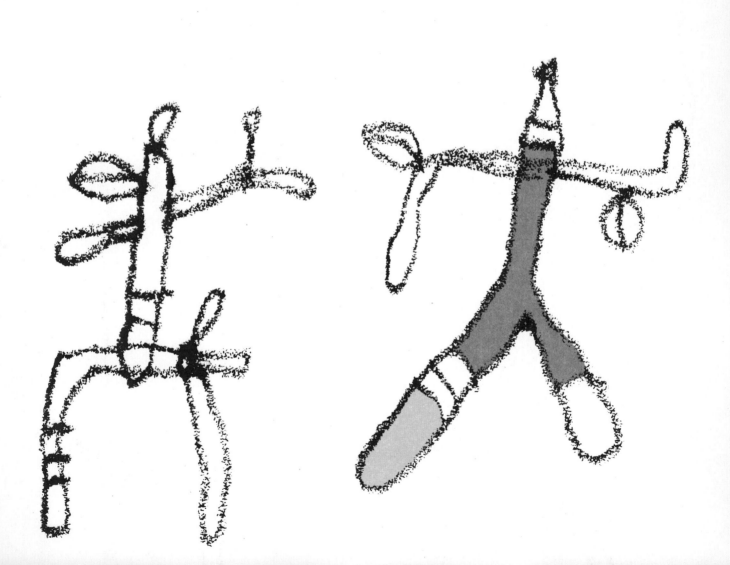

Draw the sandwich that came in this wrapper.

Fill this box with candies.

It's a field trip! Draw children in the bus.

Draw children having a picnic.

Here is a very beautiful bird.

And here is a very stylish one.

Draw people screaming with delight.

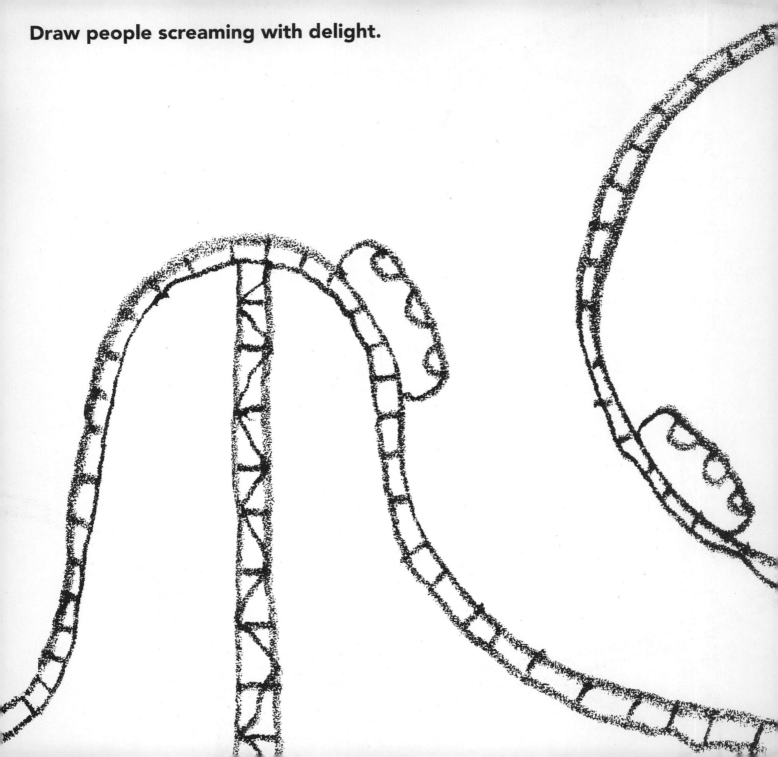

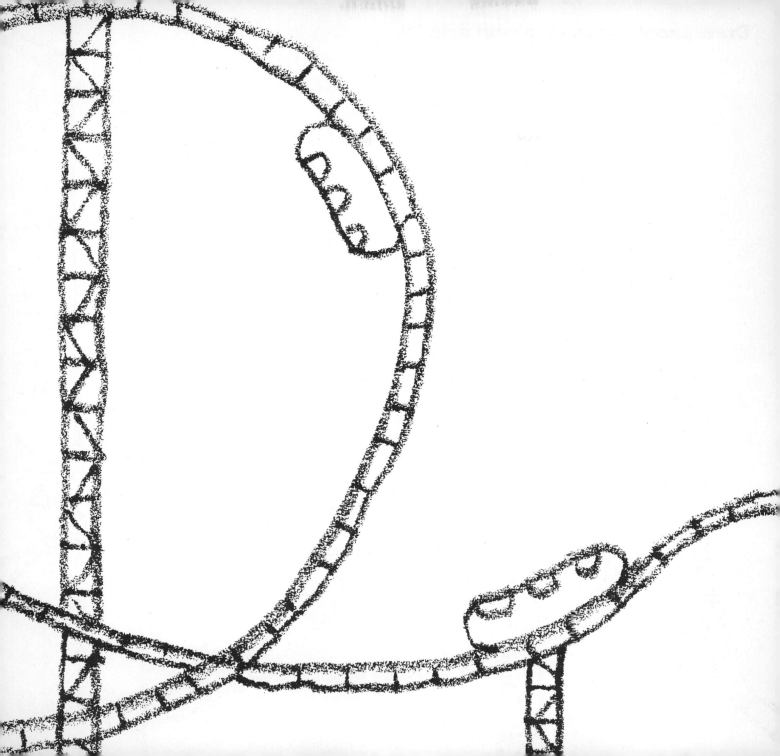

Draw a train crossing this bridge.

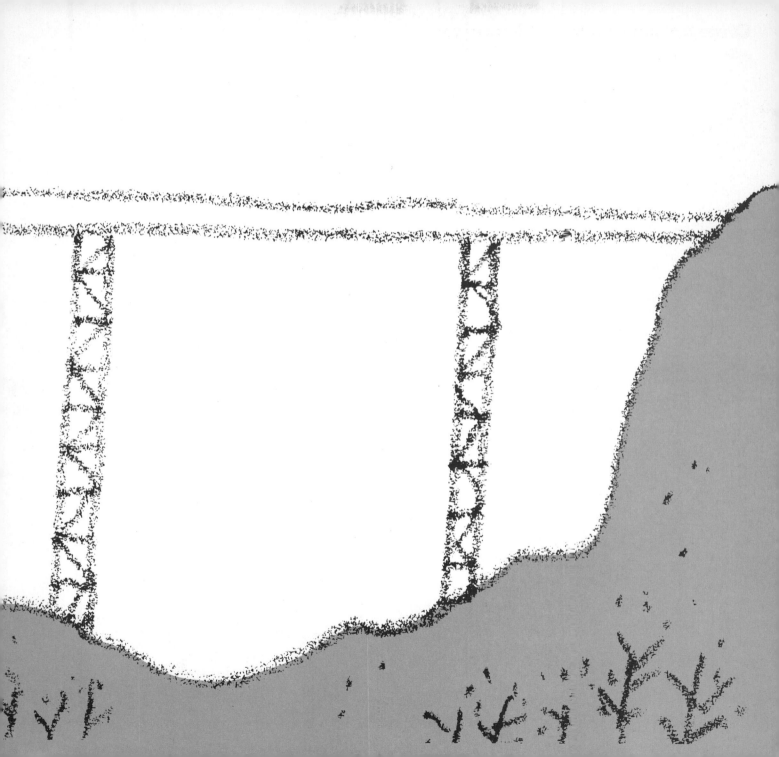

Color the chestnuts on this tree and also draw birds.

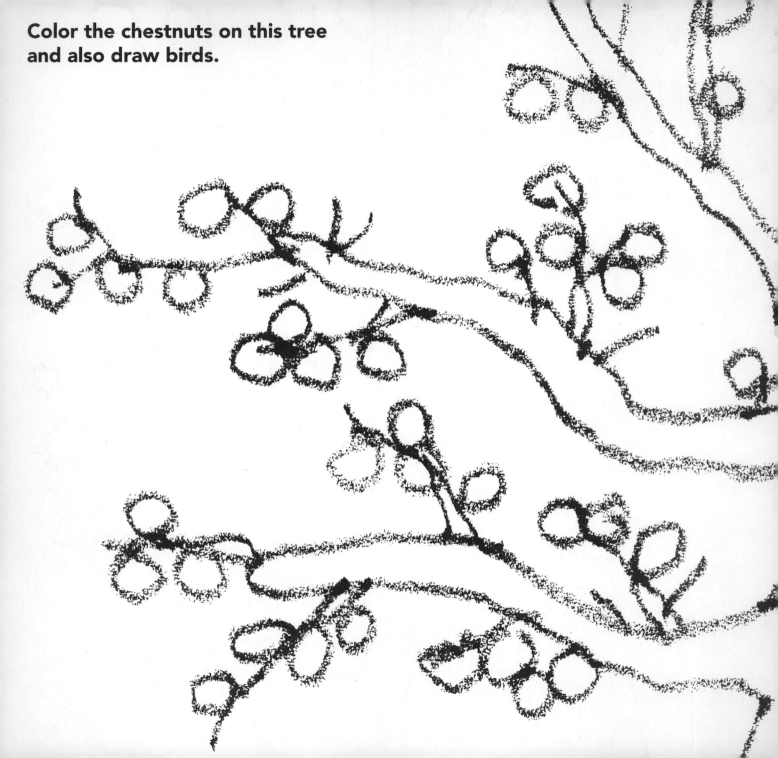

Color these dragonflies red, orange, or even pink!

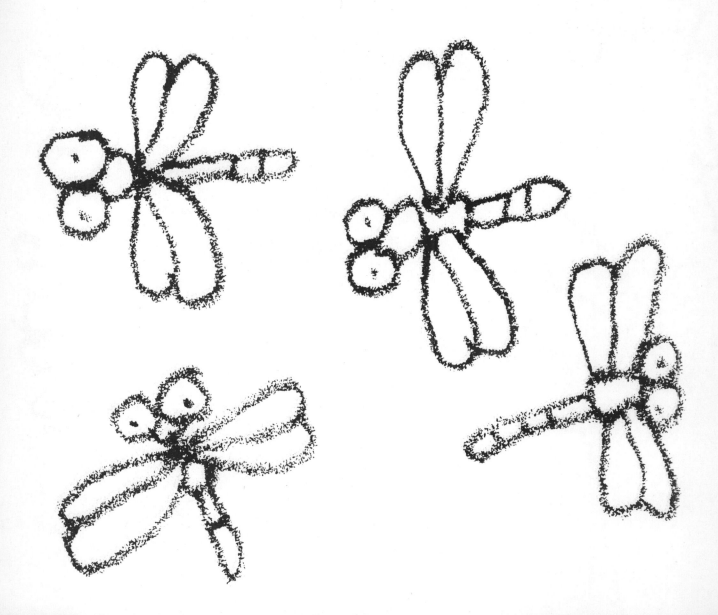

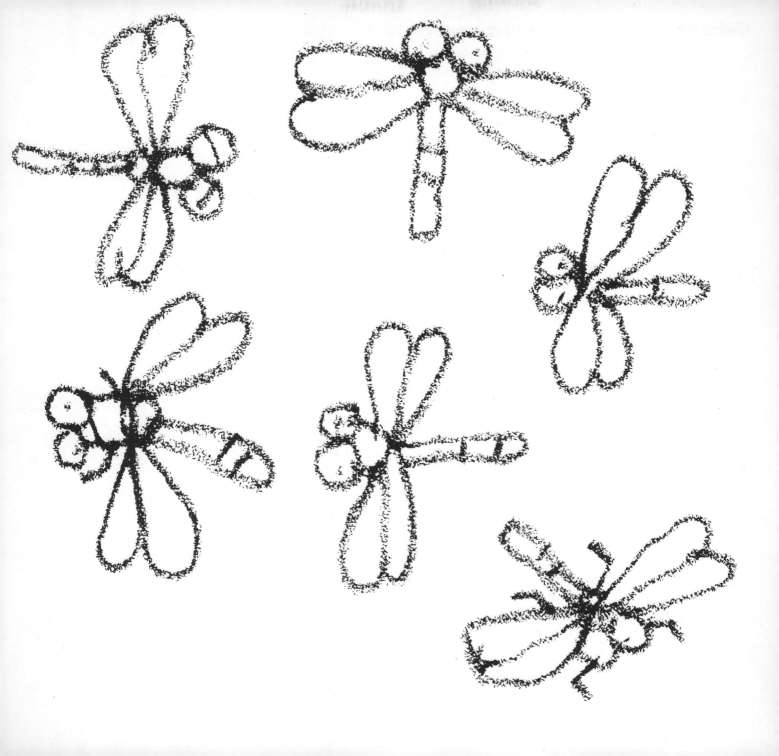

Make the dragonflies land on every post.

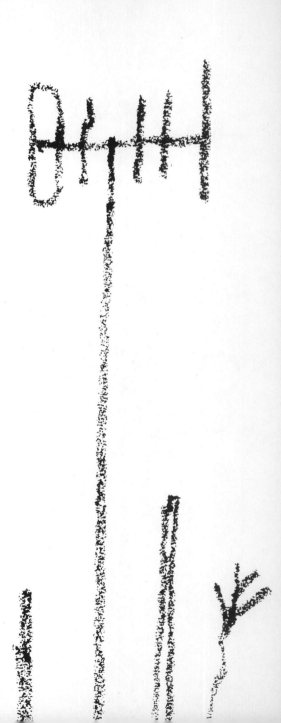

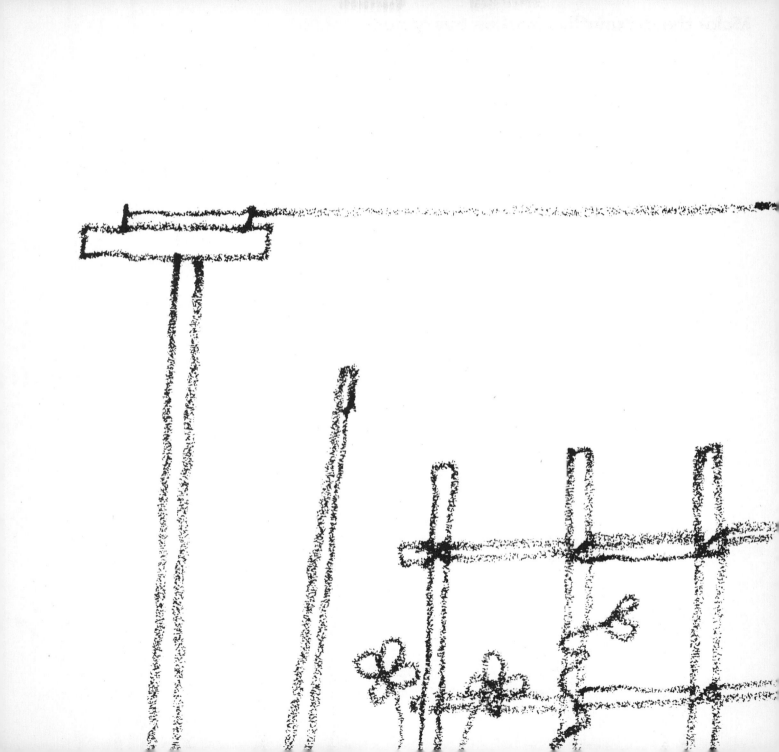

Color these leaves.

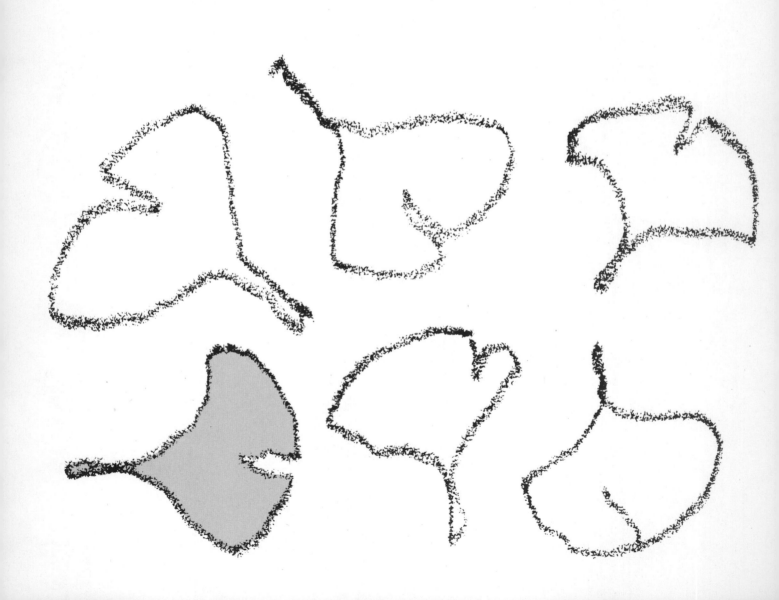

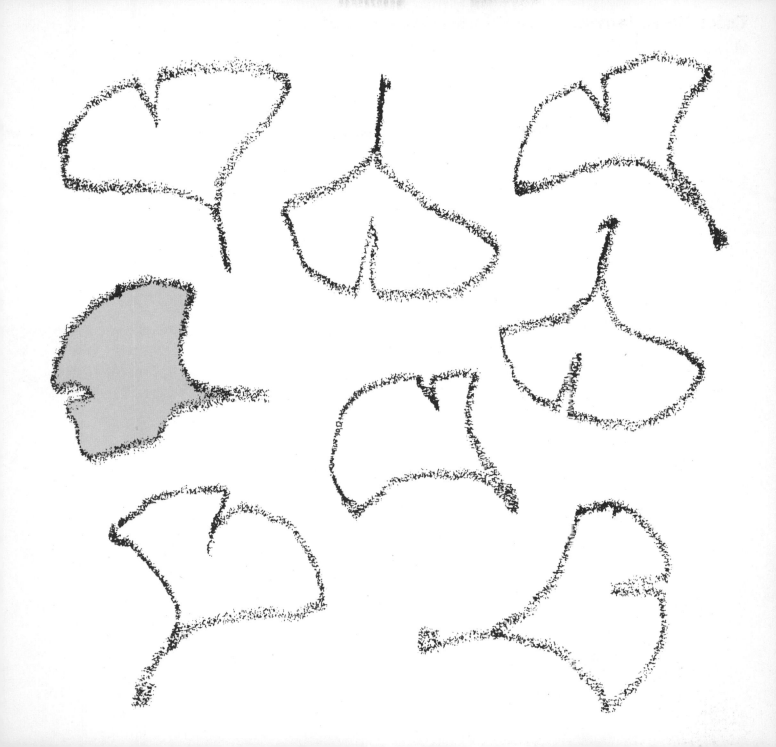

This lake is very calm. Draw some boats on it.
What would happen if the Loch Ness monster suddenly appeared?

Fill this plate with tasty food.

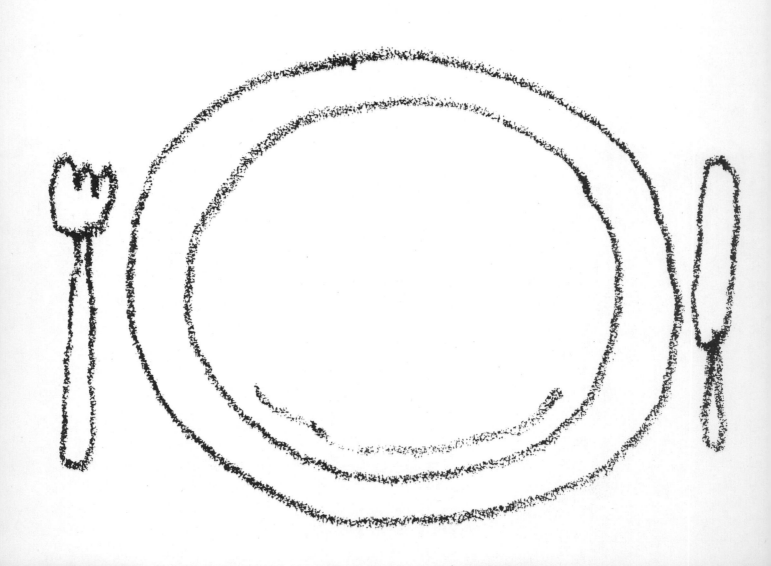

Color these grapes and draw people picking them.

Draw farmers driving tractors.

These trees need autumn leaves.

Imagine palm trees turn autumn colors, too!

And why not cactuses?

What if even the ocean changed color in the fall?

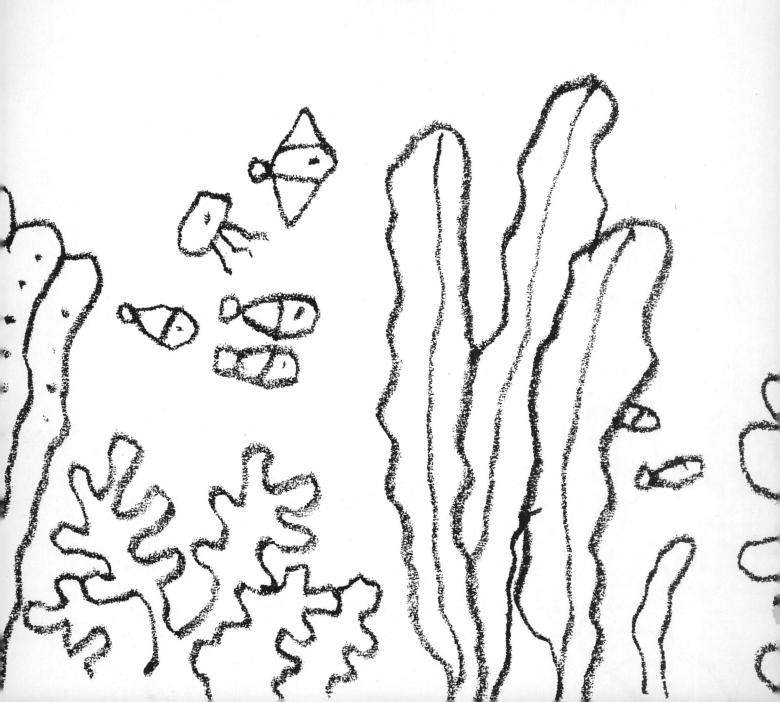

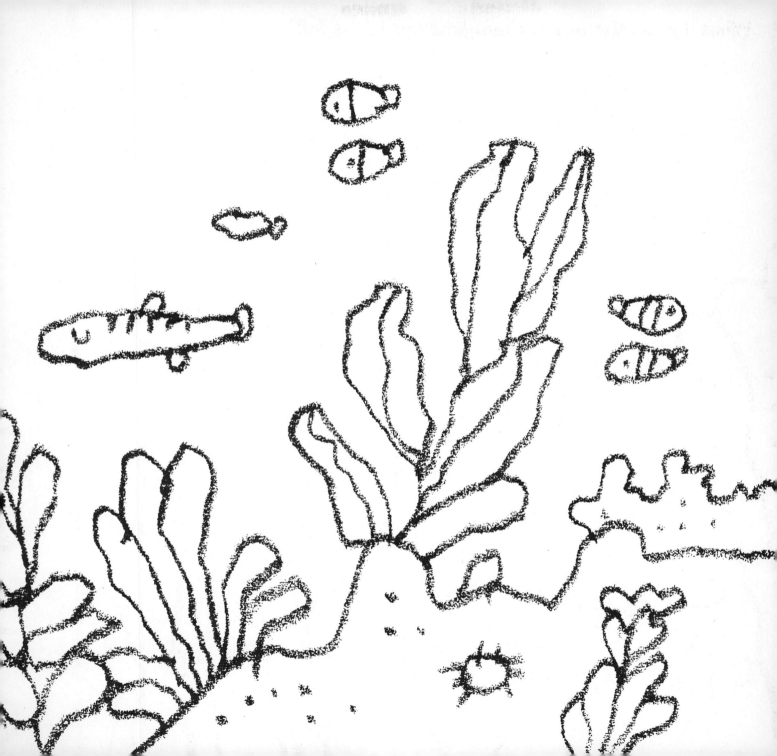

Draw warm clothes on these children.

Draw birds migrating.

Draw lots of bugs.

Color these persimmons.

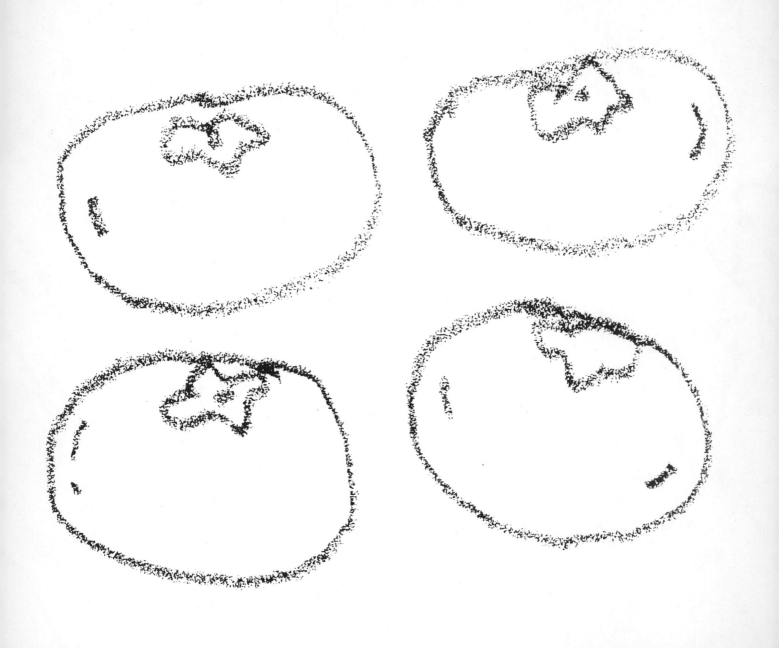

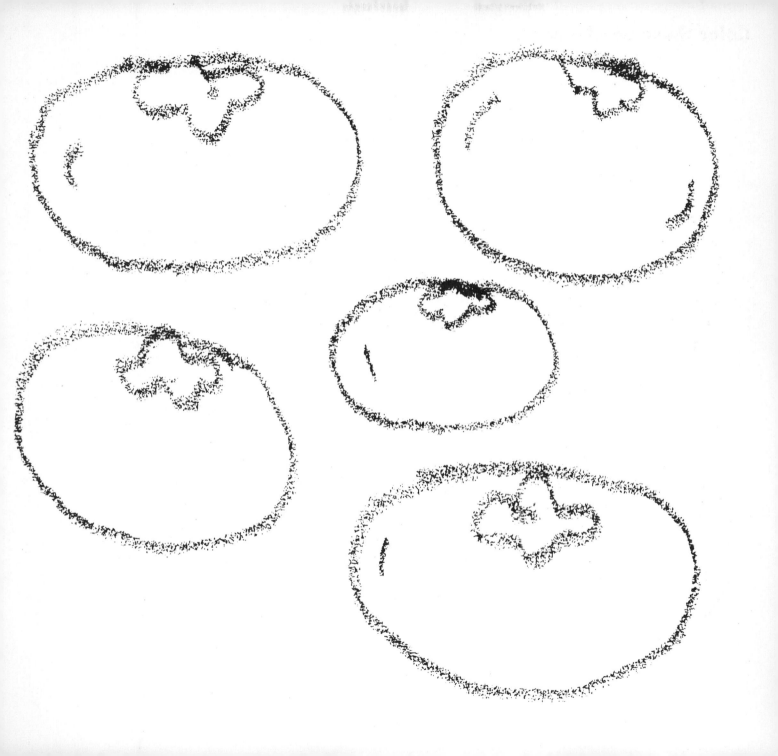

Color these chestnuts.

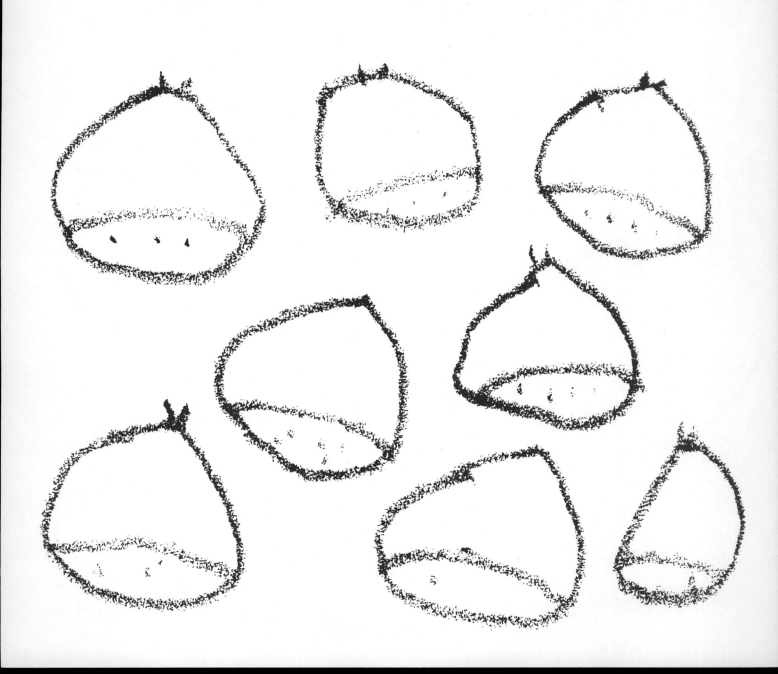

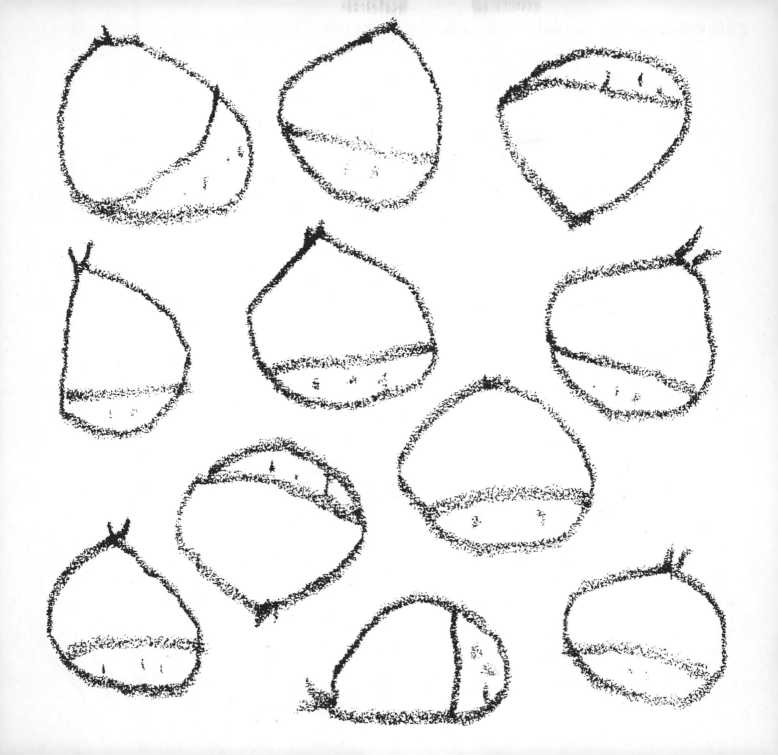

This scarecrow is lonely. Make some scarecrow friends for him.

Color these fruits, nuts, and seeds.

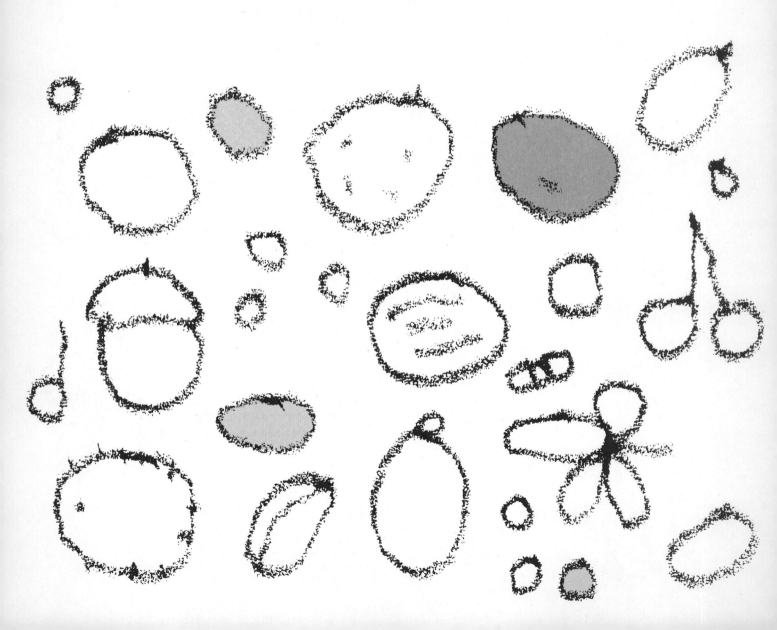

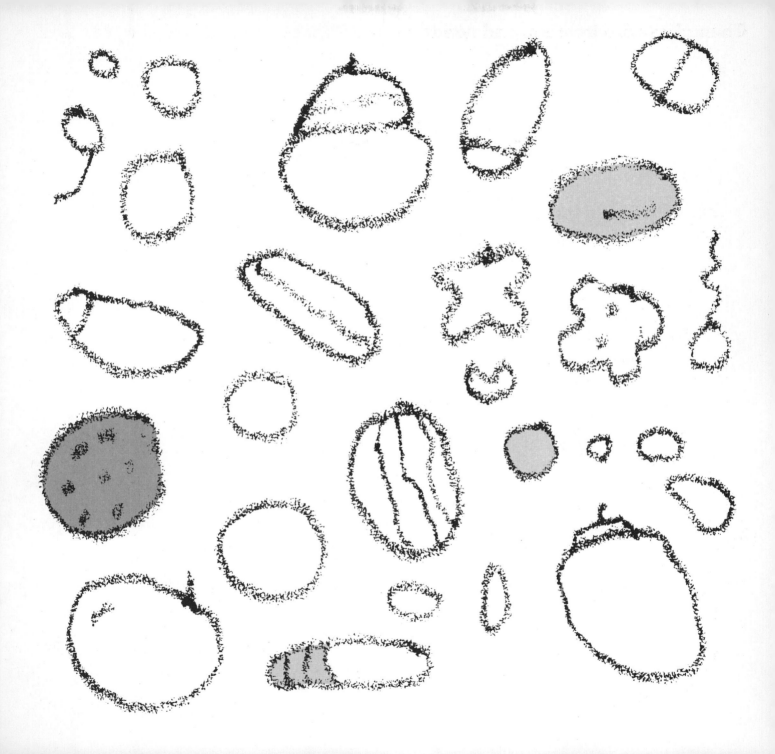

These kids are wearing Halloween masks. What creatures are they?

It's a parade! What do you think they are carrying?

Draw lots of people pulling this float.

Draw the full moon.

**Draw lots of mushrooms
on the forest floor.**

Color these mushrooms different colors.
(But be careful of the poisonous ones!)

So—what's for dinner?

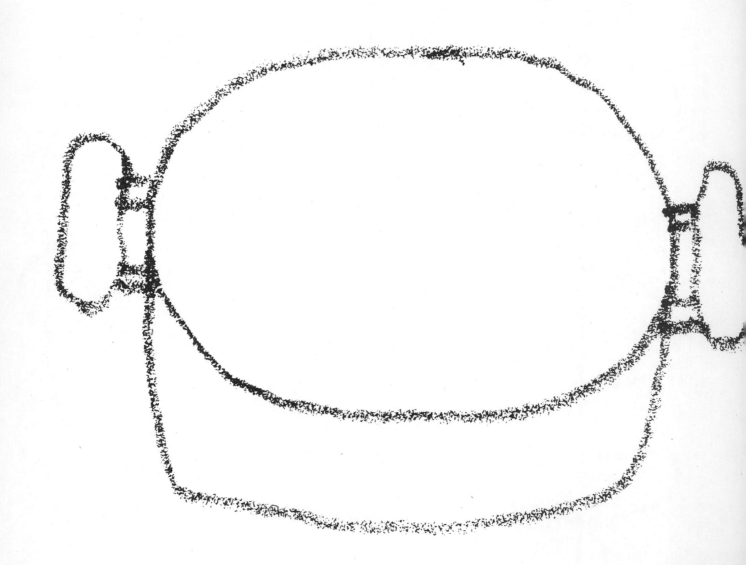

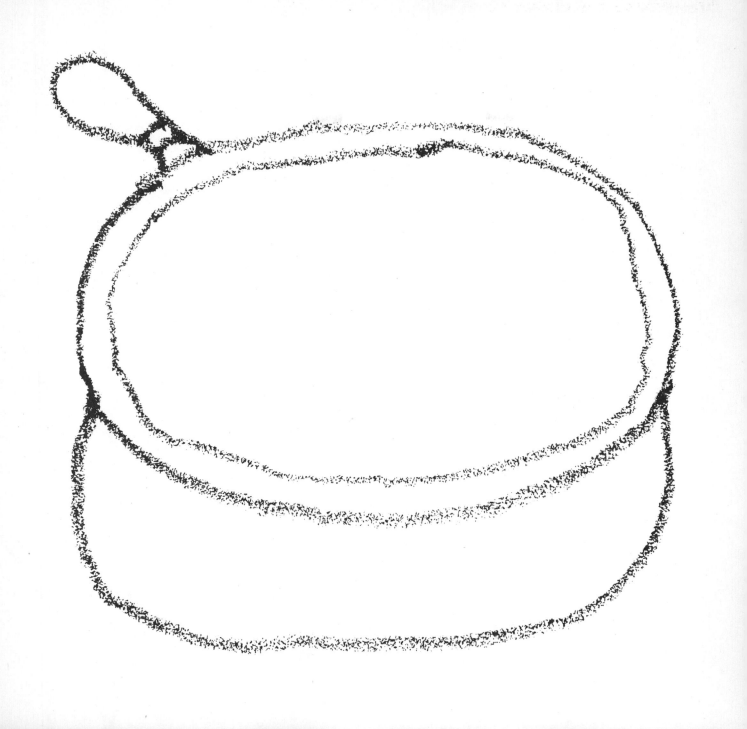

Draw cars on this mountain road.

What pretty sweaters! Draw patterns on them.

This horse needs a rider.

Color these helicopters.
(Don't forget to draw the pilots!)

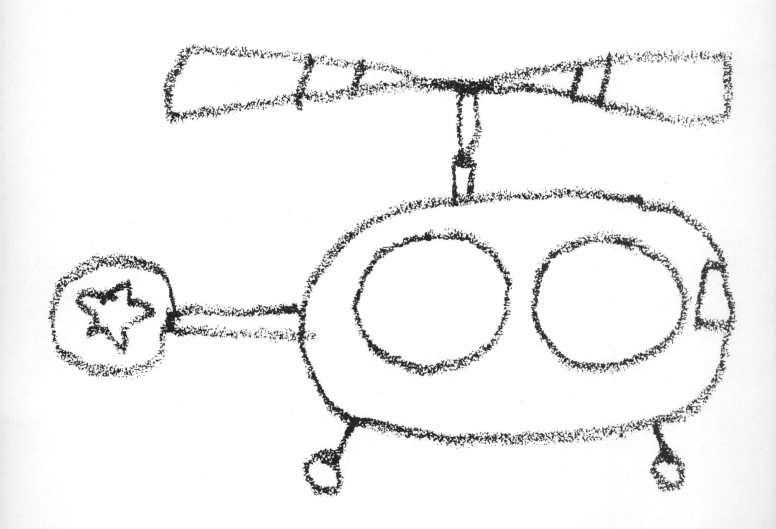

Draw an autumn sunset.

Create some constellations.
(If you can find the Little Dipper, you're a star!)

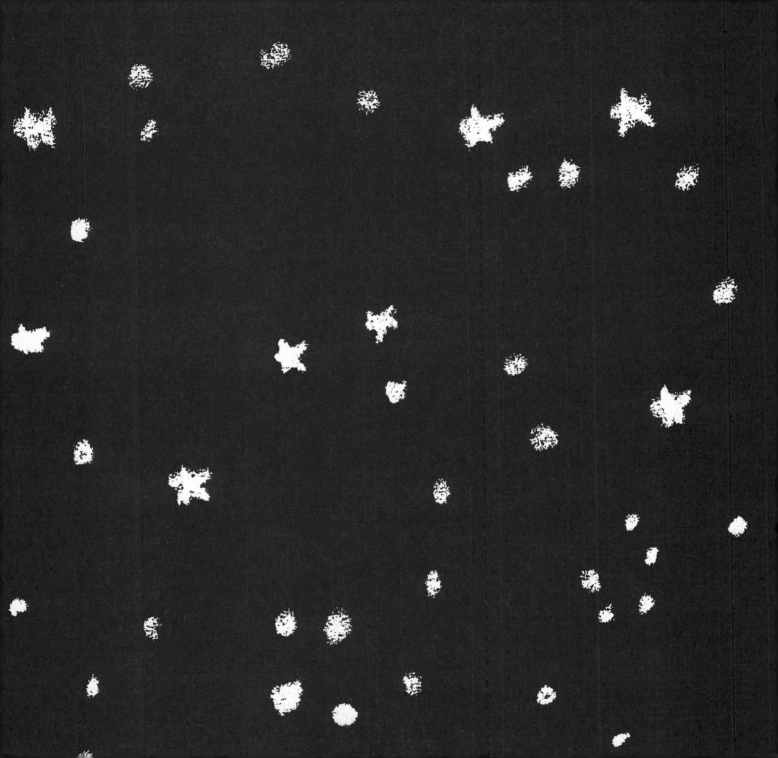

Winter is nearly here. Can you help this squirrel gather nuts to store and help this bear find food before it hibernates?

GOTTI
TANO

Winter

**Give these people warm winter clothing.
Don't forget hats!**

These people need gloves and socks.

**Draw someone who likes cold weather
and someone who doesn't.**

These animals need warm clothing, too!

So do these animals.

Build a snowman. Or a snow woman.

What kind of face does your snowman have?

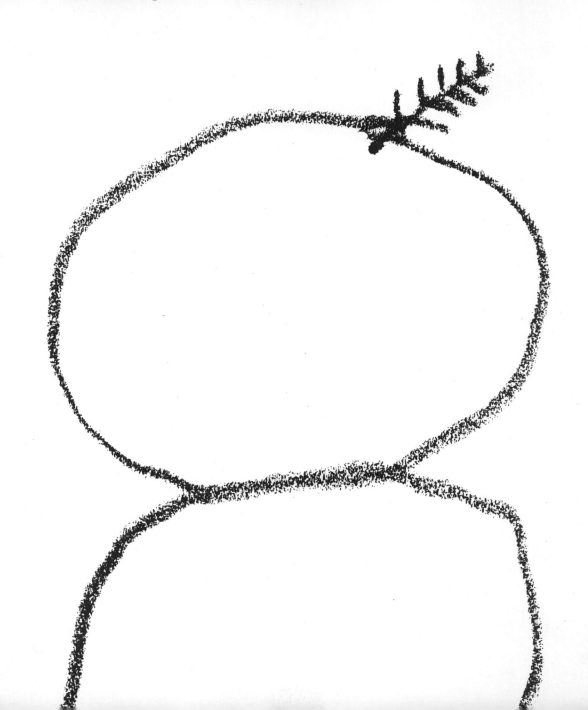

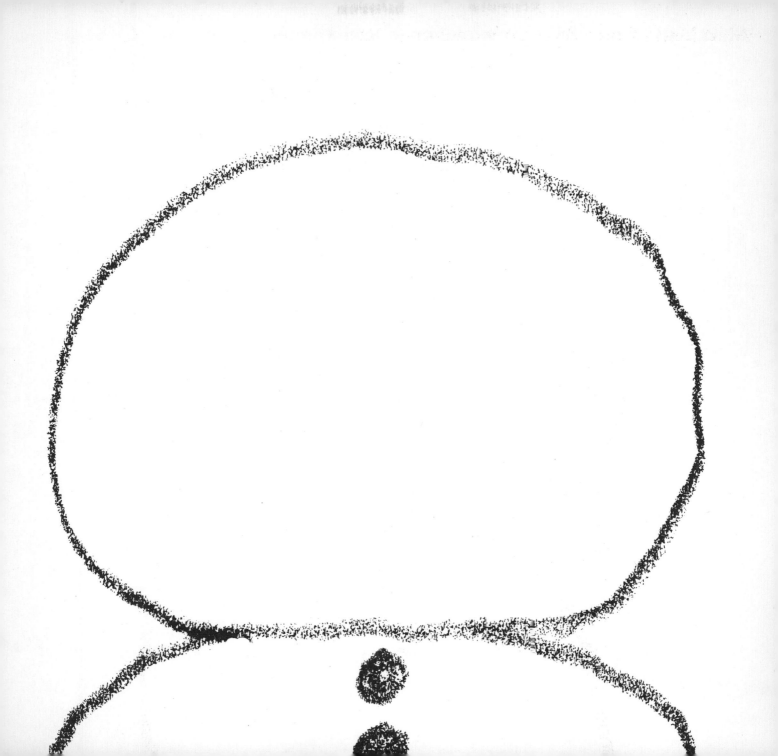

Build a snow giraffe, a snow elephant, and a snow panda.

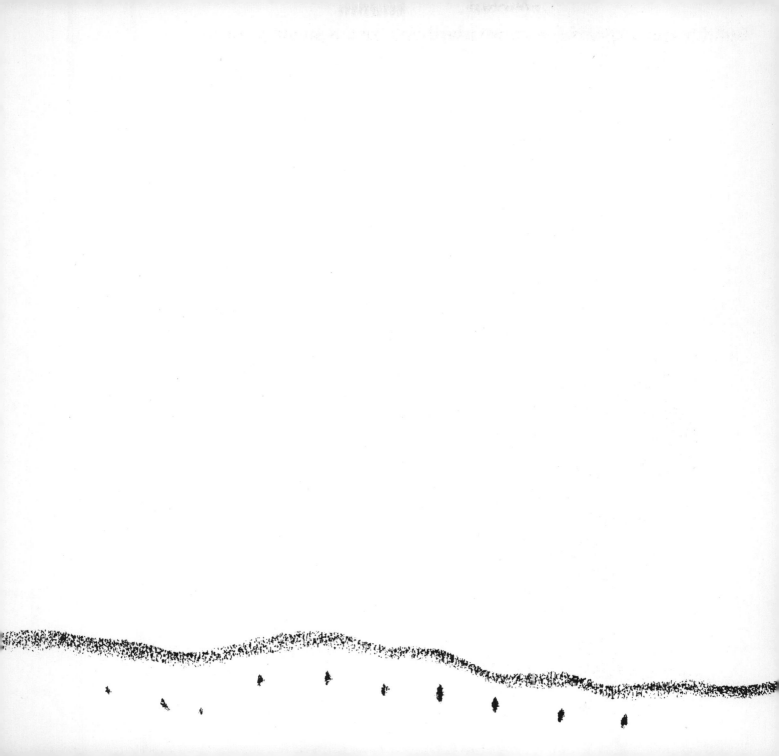

Can these children see their breath in the cold air?

Draw some more people skiing and snowboarding.

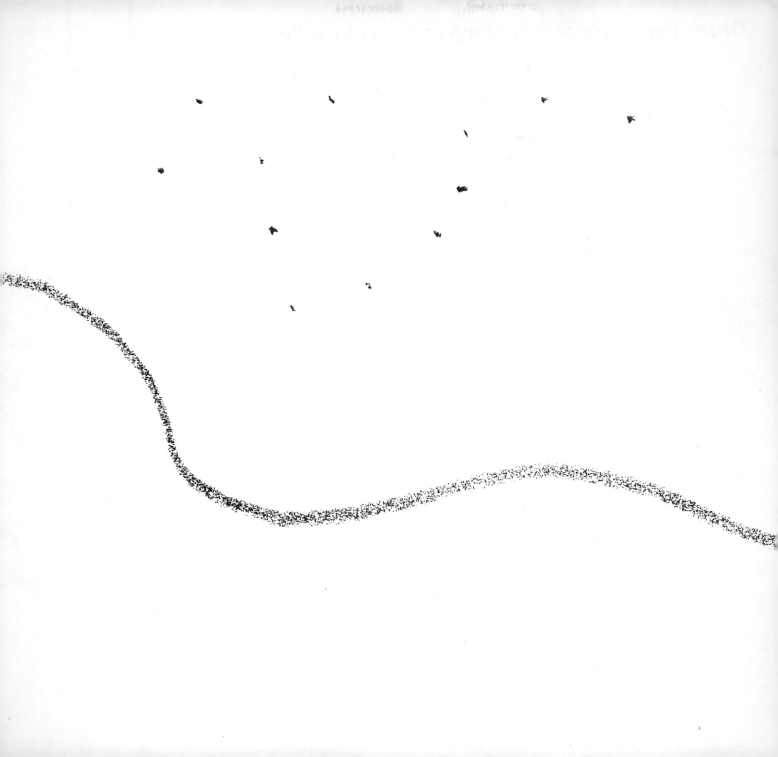

Watch out! It's a snowball fight!

Draw some more creatures hibernating.

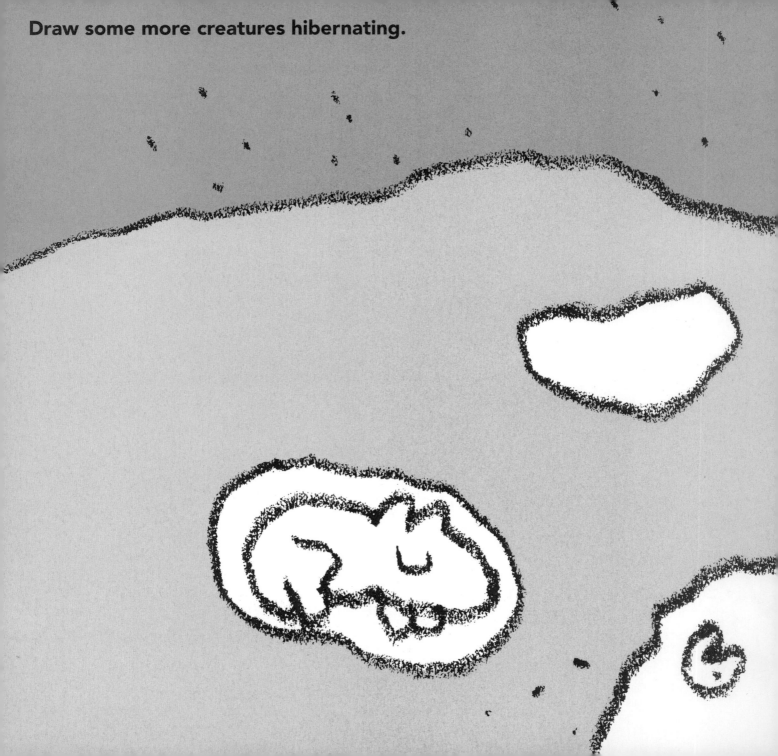

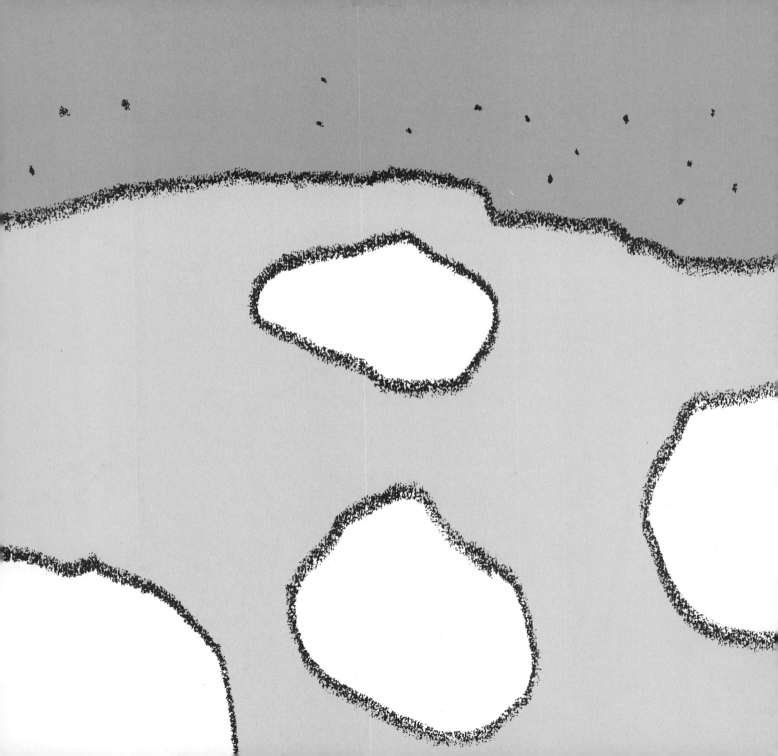

Make this room warm and cozy.

Cover these kids with warm blankets.

Light these candles.

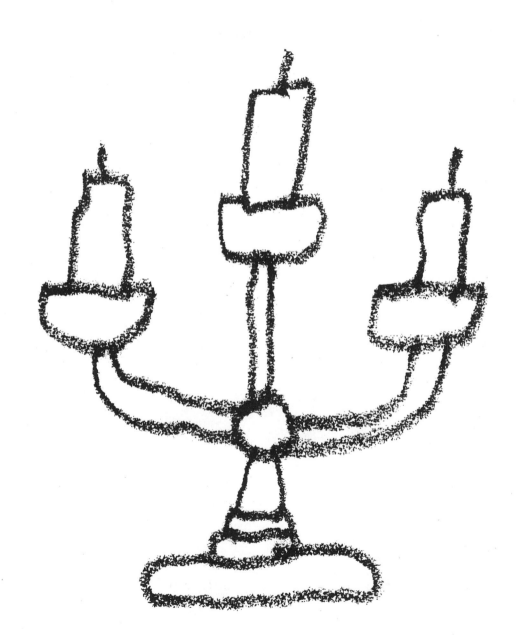

Time to decorate the tree!

What presents have been unwrapped? Who are they for?

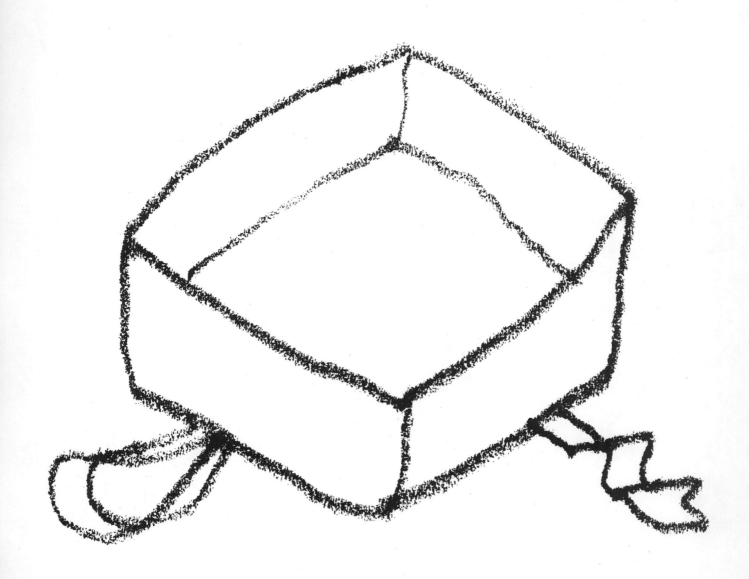

Draw a present that you'd like to get.
(Show this page to someone you'd like to give it to you.)

Can you dress up this boy as Santa Claus?

Santa needs a sled!

Draw pictures on these playing cards.

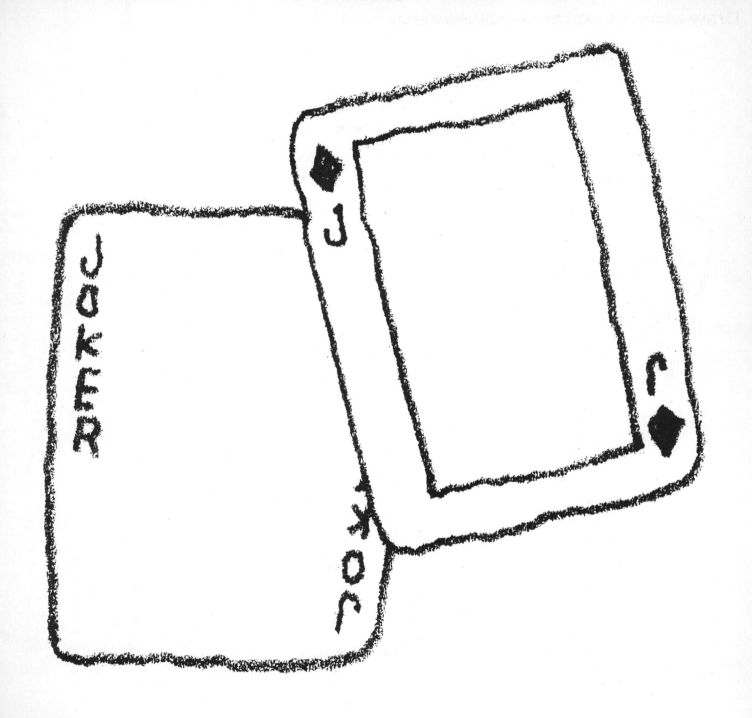

Draw someone taking a hot, relaxing bath.

It's time to ring in the New Year.
(Can you help this boy ring this bell?)

Draw a sunrise on New Year's Day.

Draw holiday decorations on this person's house.

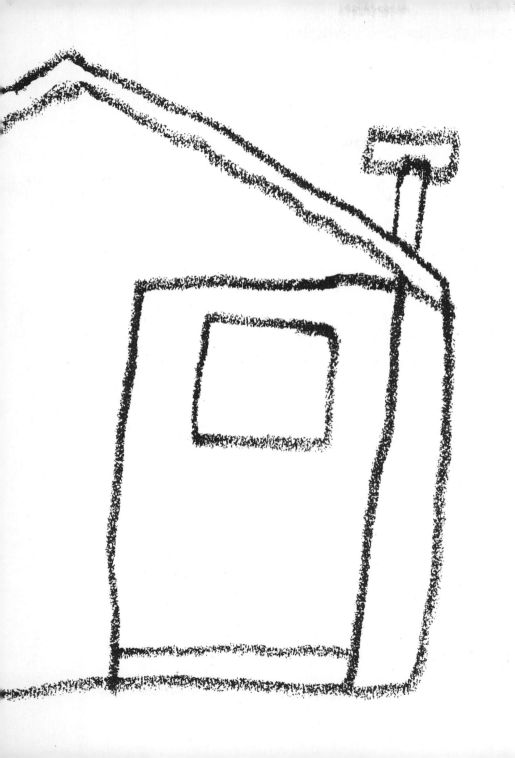

What are your New Year's resolutions? Write them here.

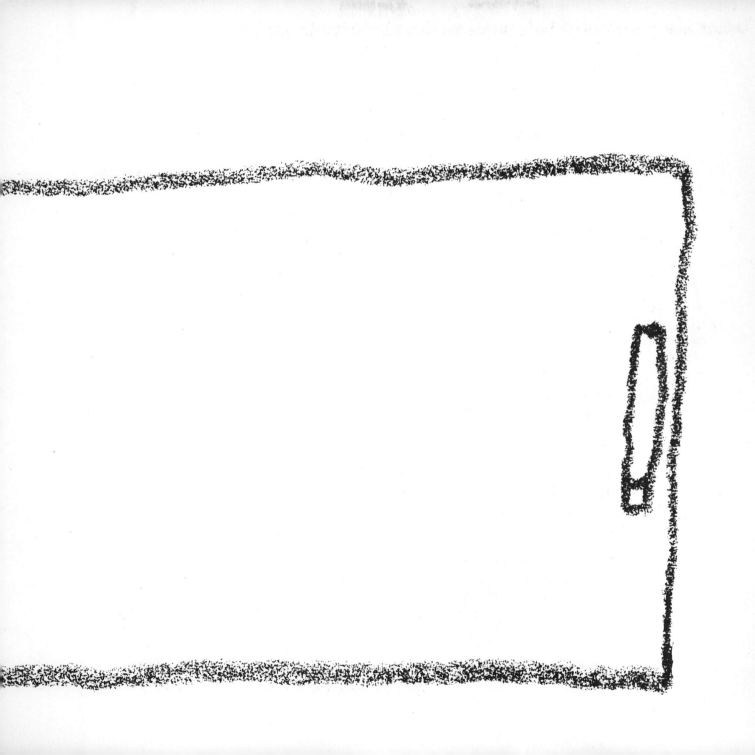

What do you think their New Year's resolutions are?

This is a little difficult, but . . . draw the face of this creature.

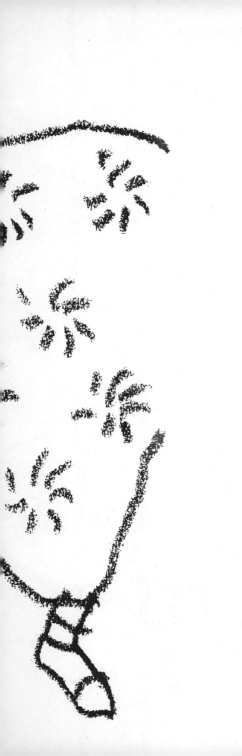

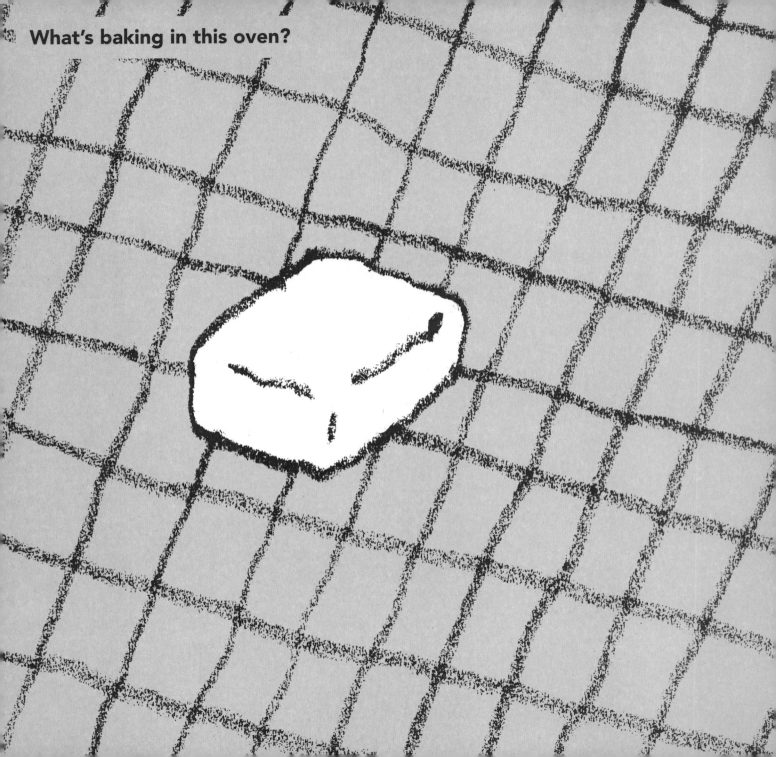

What's baking in this oven?

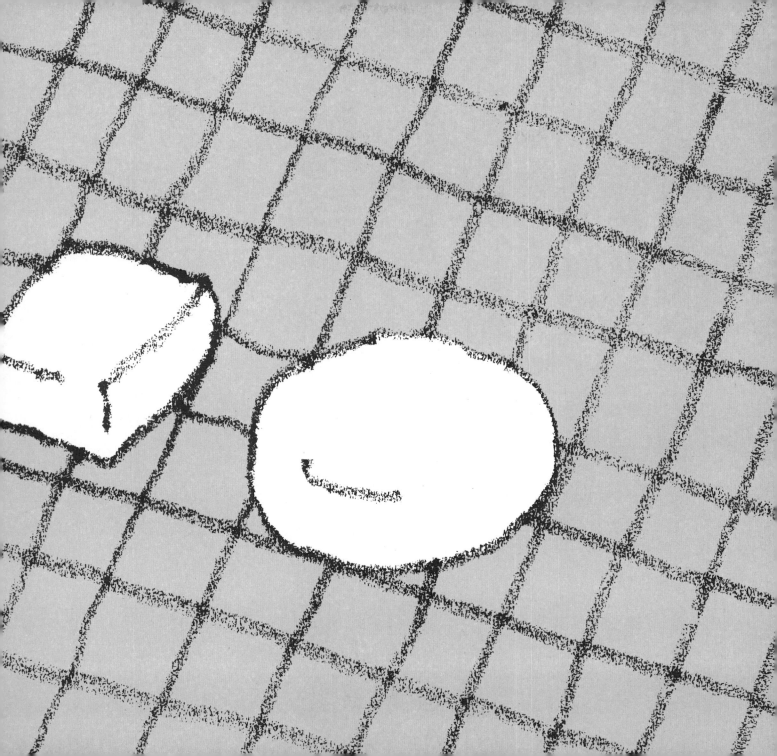

This boy needs a kite. Can you draw it?

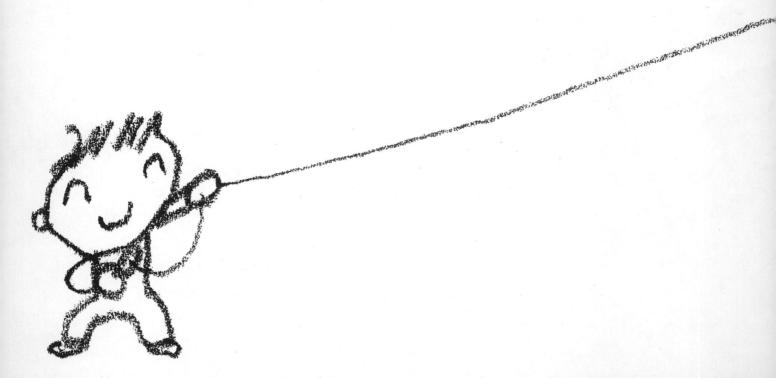

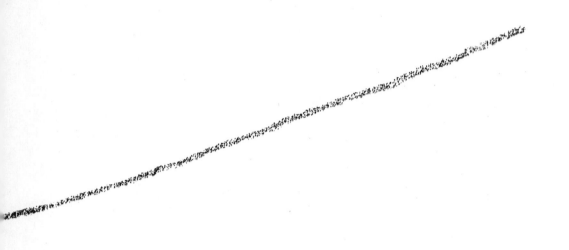

Draw funny faces on these snowmen.

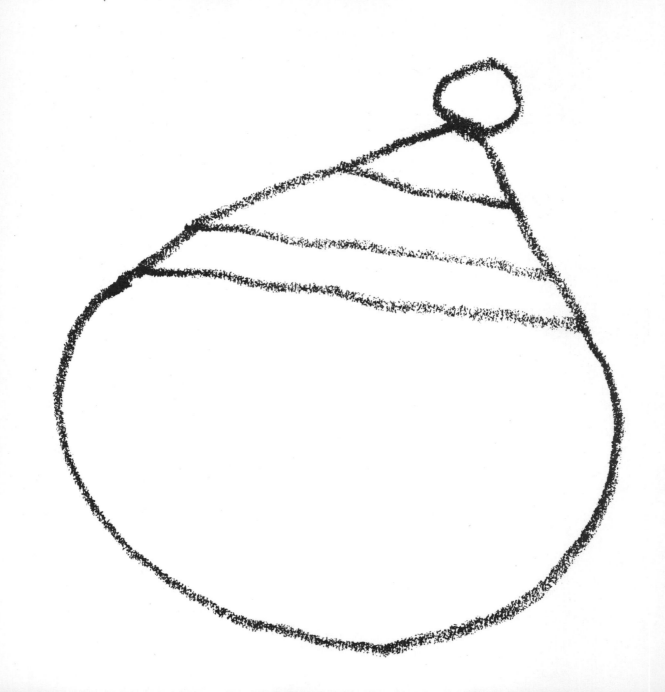

Draw some people sitting around this table.
(Don't forget their chairs!)

Cook something delicious.

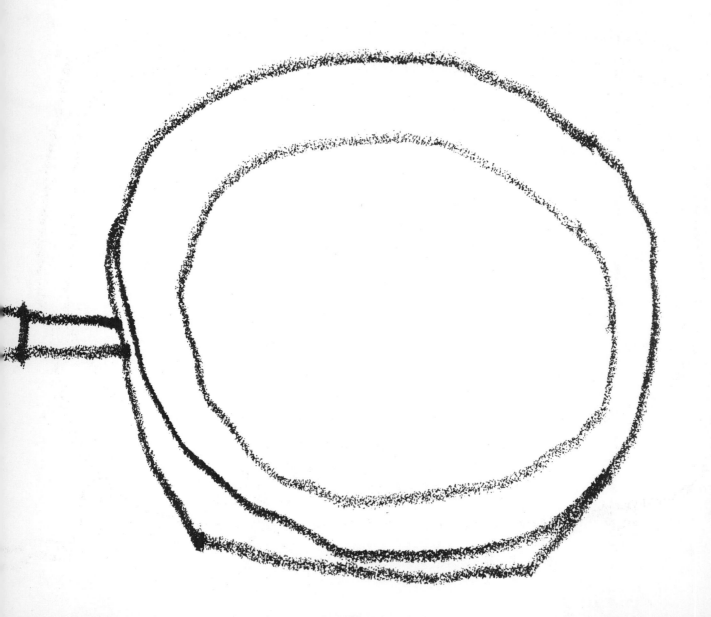

Draw a lollipop for this boy.

What do you think this snow is covering?

Draw a winter rainbow.

Draw more ice-skaters.

These people need warm coats.

So do these creatures.

Draw people enjoying the winter weather.

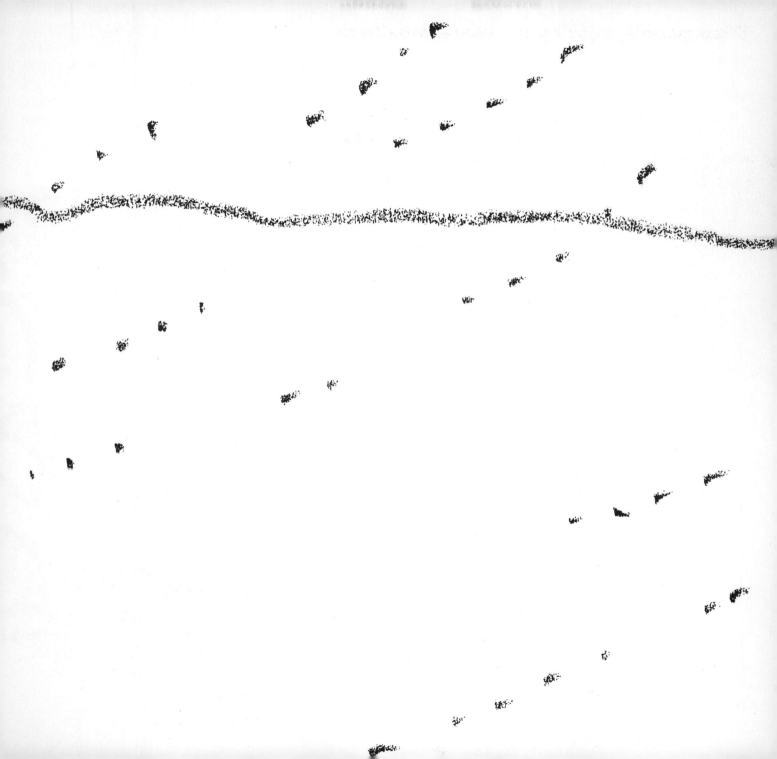

What game is this? Draw some more players.

Here are some igloos. Draw people inside them.

Draw some constellations in the winter sky.
(If you can find Orion, you're a star!)

Spring is coming soon! Draw the first flower buds.

Gomi ✳ Taro

Taro Gomi was born in Tokyo in 1945. In his very long career, he has created more than 350 books for readers of all ages. His work has been translated into more than 15 languages, and among the 30 of his books to be published outside of Japan are **Everyone Poops, My Friends, Spring Is Here, Scribbles,** and **Doodles.**

This edition published in 2009 exclusively for Starbucks Coffee Company by Chronicle Books LLC.

Original edition published in Japan by Bronze Publishing Inc., Tokyo, under the title *Itudemo Rakugaki*.

English type design by Wendy Lui.
Typeset in Avenir.
Manufactured in Singapore.

ISBN: 978-9-8118-7179-2

10 9 8 7 6 5 4 3 2 1

Chronicle Books LLC
680 Second Street
San Francisco, CA 94107

www.chroniclebooks.com/custom